Old, Bold and Won't Be Told

Old, Bold and Won't Be Told

Shakespeare's Amazing Ageing Ladies

Yvonne Oram

THAMES RIVER PRESS

Old, Bold and Won't Be Told

THAMES RIVER PRESS
An imprint of Wimbledon Publishing Company Limited (WPC)
Another imprint of WPC is Anthem Press (www.anthempress.com)
First published in the United Kingdom in 2013 by
THAMES RIVER PRESS
75–76 Blackfriars Road
London SE1 8HA

www.thamesriverpress.com

A CIP record for this book is available from the British Library.

ISBN 978-0-85728-203-3

Cover design by Sylwia Palka

This title is also available as an eBook

*To all the amazing ageing ladies in my life for their inspiration
and to Steve and Ivor for their unfailing
encouragement and support*

CONTENTS

ACKNOWLEDGEMENTS

This book began life as research for my PhD at the Shakespeare Institute, University of Birmingham, and I thank my supervisor, Dr Martin Wiggins, for the intellectual focus which kept me on track; the Shakespeare Institute Library staff, who were unfailingly helpful and good-humoured; all the members of the Renaissance Studies Group, and Yvonne Steinmetz-Ardaseer, fellow student and friend. And I'm grateful to Bridget Carrick, Jacky Humby, Lili Sanchez and Trish Woods for their encouragement over the years.

The work has developed as lectures for conferences at Shakespeare's Globe, London, and the University of Reading, and as contributions to study events at Literature and History Societies here and abroad.

I have drawn upon material from my essay, 'Representations of Ageing Female Rulers on the Early Modern Stage' in *Representations of Elizabeth I in Early Modern Culture*, edited by Alessandra Petrina and Laura Tosi (Palgrave Macmillan, 2011), reproduced with permission.

INTRODUCTION

In 1610 Shakespeare created a rich role for an ageing woman; the character of Paulina in *The Winter's Tale*. She is crucial to the story – particularly to the almost magical events and family reconciliations in the final scene – and she's unique among the many older women portrayed on stage during the Elizabethan and Jacobean periods in that she maintains active, dramatic centrality until the very end of the play.

Though none of them quite matches the powerful Paulina there are other thoroughly engaging old women (both good and bad) in Shakespeare's plays. However, it's important to be aware that Shakespeare, like his fellow playwrights, often depicts the old woman critically, reflecting socially approved models of good behaviour along with deep anxieties about bad behaviour, for the ageing ladies of his day. He also presents onstage male methods of schooling unseemly conduct. On the 'good' side the old woman is usually imaged as guiding, counselling and supportive (often in a maternal role) and on the 'bad' as a butt of comedy or a source of discomfort because of her loss of looks, inappropriate sexual desires, verbal incontinence and potential for dangerous behaviour. Only Shakespeare moves beyond these good and bad dramatic stereotypes, though, in creating a handful of women who are old and bold and certainly won't be told what to do. They challenge male authority and Shakespeare celebrates such defiance, highlighting the creativity of the old woman. This book explores these ageing women in detail – they are the two wives in *The Merry Wives of Windsor* (1597–98); Gertrude in *Hamlet* (1600–1601); Cleopatra in *Antony and Cleopatra* (1606); Volumnia in *Coriolanus* (1608) and Katherine of Aragon in *Henry VIII: All Is True* (1613). However, Paulina is the finest example for, in presenting her audience with the dramatic 'reincarnation' of the supposedly dead Queen Hermione, she becomes the creator and director of her own production – the female equivalent of the man who made her up. Of course, Shakespeare's play is just a far-fetched 'tale of romantic improbability' which even the practical Paulina feels is likely to 'be hooted at' (5.3.117).[1] Yet her role in it is special. Her character was added by Shakespeare to the original storyline taken from Robert Greene's *Pandosto: The Triumph of Time* (c.1588) and at the very end of *The Winter's Tale* Paulina is still alive, articulate, a free woman and acknowledged as powerful by the dominant male character in the drama – 'Good Paulina, lead us from hence [...]' (5.3.152). This marks a startling break with Early Modern dramatic convention with regard to the old woman.

It is important to note that this book is not a guide as to how these characters should be played on stage – though I hope my ideas are interesting to the modern female actor moving into maturity.[2] Rather, I consider the various ways of writing the ageing woman in the plays of Shakespeare and his contemporary dramatists, in relation to the activities of such women in Elizabethan and Jacobean society. My exploration of play texts is set alongside historical evidence and I refer to the work of a number of social historians as well as scholars of Early Modern drama. My aim is to make my findings accessible to academic and non-academic readers alike.

The first section of this study engages with conventional characterisations and I look at the main dramatic stereotypes of the ageing woman onstage in the Elizabethan and Jacobean periods. These focused on her loss of looks, her unbridled sexuality and her inability to keep her mouth shut. Here, and throughout the book, Shakespeare's work is considered alongside publicly performed plays by

---

1 John Jowett, William Montgomery, Gary Taylor and Stanley Wells, eds, *The Oxford Shakespeare: The Complete Works*. 2nd edn (Oxford: Clarendon Press, 2006), 1123.

2 In 2010 two mature female actors were cast against age expectations in Shakespeare's plays – Judi Dench as Titania in *A Midsummer Night's Dream*, directed by Peter Hall and Siân Phillips as Juliet in *Juliet and Her Romeo*, directed by Tom Morris. In the same year Helen Mirren was a female Prospero in the film of *The Tempest*, directed by Julie Taymor. Previously, Kathryn Hunter played *King Lear* in the 1997 production directed by Helena Haut-Howson.

dramatists of the same period but I have limited this study to roughly the period of his 'working life' as a dramatist, considering that by 1614 his 'career was virtually at an end'.[3] My exploration and comparison of plays is always based upon analysis of the language of the plays used by the playwrights concerned.

It will be clear that the drama of the day depicted most of the older women as functioning only within the private sphere of home and family, yet historical records challenge this. During the reigns of Elizabeth I and her successor James Stuart old women were not only busy within the family circle but were also out and about and active in almost all areas of society; I look at historical material engaging with all aspects of the older woman's life – indoors and out.

I go on to consider the stereotypical stage characters of old women whose actions and behaviour set a perfect example, including devoted mothers and loyal wives, as well as old women who offer guidance, support and counselling. I then move to those who are depicted as being in serious need of controlling measures from their menfolk: the disobedient, the lustful and the power hungry. Here I also consider the stage bawd – that most socially subversive of old women – and her counterpart within the family, the ageing nurse.

The final part of this study considers the old women named above, Shakespeare's mature female characters who subvert the stereotypes, concluding with his most amazing ageing lady, Paulina. It's interesting to see that in creating this character Shakespeare glances at all the dramatic stereotypes connected to the old woman. At the start of the play Paulina is a caring mother figure to her mistress, the wronged Queen Hermione, but is also mocked as a disobedient wife. Widowed when her husband falls foul of a passing bear she becomes a rigorous counsellor and guide to the widowed King Leontes yet there is a touch of bawdiness in her sensual reminiscing with him (5.1.19–55) and in her presentation of the statue in Act 5 scene 3. However, throughout the play Paulina evades all stereotyping and finally achieves autonomy

---

3 Stanley Wells, *Shakespeare & Co.* (London: Penguin, 2007), 156.

as the independent creator of a happy ending for the 'precious winners all' (5.3.132).

It's clear that 'In each historical era the praise of old age and ageism [...] existed side by side'.[4] The experience and the experiences of old age are important to any society but we tend not to engage with these until we're old ourselves and certainly our own society could pay much more attention to the positive aspects of ageing, rather than being so scared of the negative side of this inevitable state. Shakespeare's plays place him in the positive camp, though not consistently nor continually for he was often content to access stereotypes of old women for his plays. However, when he did work innovatively with these characters it was in ways which value and promote the on-going strength and creativity of the old and ageing woman.

---

4 Daniel Schafer, 'Medical Representations of Old Age in the Renaissance: The Influence of Non-Medical Texts' in *Growing Old in Early Modern Europe Cultural Representations*, ed. Erin Campbell (Aldershot: Ashgate, 2006), 11–19, 12.

Part I

EARLY MODERN OLD WOMEN – ONSTAGE AND OFF

Old Women Onstage: Not a Pretty Sight?

> Hermione was not so much wrinkled, nothing
> So aged as this seems.
>
> *The Winter's Tale*, 5.3.28–29

The immediate reaction of Leontes when faced with the 'statue' of the wife he hasn't seen for 16 years is to exclaim at her loss of looks. And while this alerts us to the possibility of sculptural chicanery (the statue later comes to life) his response also typifies male antipathy towards the visible effects of female ageing. This is often shown far less subtly as distaste and derision in Early Modern drama and Shakespeare's plays are no exception. In *Richard III* (1592–93) the old Lancastrian matriarch Queen Margaret is described as a 'foul, wrinkled witch' (1.3.164), while Lear's vituperative cursing of his daughter Goneril in *King Lear* (1610) includes the fond hope that any child she has will 'stamp wrinkles in her brow of youth' (1.4.263). Clearly, wrinkles were problematic well before moisturisers hit the market place in a big way. However, general signs of decay were also targeted in literature. In his comic poem on the ages of women, Thomas Tusser refers tartly to 'trim beauty' falling off rapidly as women turn into 'matrons or drudges'.[1]

But was it just those tell-tale outward signs which caused a woman to be labelled as old in Shakespeare's day? Fifty was often marked as

---

1 Thomas Tusser, 'Description of Woman's Age by VI Times XIII Years Prenticeship, With a Lesson to the Same' (1562), in *Chaste, Silent and Obedient: English Books for Women 1475–1640*, ed. Suzanne W. Hull (San Marino: Huntington Library, 1962), 65.

'the end of adult maturity and the start of old age, though not necessarily the start of decrepitude'.[2] Early Modern dramatists don't always indicate the age of a character but a reliable onstage guide is when the woman is designated old by her own account or by the unbiased witness of others. And it's a fair assumption that she's an ageing woman if she has children of her own who are of marriageable age. Very few women married as young as Shakespeare's 14-year-old Juliet. The fact that he refers specifically to her youth in the exchanges between her mother and her nurse in *Romeo and Juliet* (1595) Act 1 scene 3 suggests that he needs to establish Juliet as unusually young to be a potential bride, for the benefit of an audience more used to the marriage conventions of their own society. This is supported by detailed work on parish registers, where analysis establishes 'a mean age of marriage for women of about 26' for the majority of the population.[3]

It's also difficult to assess how women in Shakespeare's day felt about getting old. Although old age 'has long been predominantly a female experience'[4] men were the ones who wrote about its attendant pros and cons.[5] However, there are examples of the pressures upon women to deny the ageing process, most notably in the public appearances of Queen Elizabeth I. The monarch took great pains to present herself as ever young, despite all evidence to the contrary. Paul Hentzer, a German visitor to London, records seeing the Queen 'in the 65th year of her age

---

2 Margaret Pelling, 'Old Age, Poverty and Disability in Early Modern Norwich: Work, Re-marriage and Other Expedients', in *Life, Death and the Elderly: Historical Perspectives*, ed. Margaret Pelling and Richard M. Smith (London: Routledge, 1991), 74–101 (137). There is also a useful discussion of the age issue in Dorothea Faith Kehler, 'Shakespeare's Widows of a Certain Age: Celibacy and Economics', *MHRA Working Papers in the Humanities* 1 (2006): 17–30, 19–20.

3 Ralph A. Houlbrooke, *The English Family 1450–1700* (London: Longman, 1984), 63.

4 Pat Thane, *Old Age In English History: Past Experiences, Present Issues* (Oxford: Oxford University Press, 2000), 3.

5 See for example, Henry Cuffe, *The Difference of the Ages of Man's Life* (1607); Symon Goulart, *The Wise Veillard*, translated into English in 1621; and John Reading, *The Old Man's Staffe: Two Sermons, Showing the Only Way to a Comfortable Old Age* (1621).

[...] very majestic; her face oblong, fair but wrinkled'.[6] Yet there are 'amazing images of Elizabeth painted by Nicholas Hilliard [...] in the last decade of her reign' depicting the Queen as a young girl, as well as her 'rejuvenated face' in the famous Rainbow Portrait of c.1600.[7] Those wretched wrinkles were obviously a matter of concern to even a 'very majestic' woman. As Elizabeth approached the menopause she began receiving timepieces – 'a new kind of gift [...] to be worn on her body'.[8] This fashion for giving women the means of measuring time in this way increased during the Early Modern period and could certainly carry negative imagery – 'the aged crone emblematized the body clock gone wrong: disordered, intemperate, injuring man'.[9] This view of the timepiece gift as a wake-up call for women is convincing. What better means of controlling ageing women with their problematic bodies than the use of time itself, the passing of which can so alter the physical attractions of youth? Instead of valuing, even celebrating their changing physicality women themselves will come to see all alteration in negative terms through internalisation of male standards of what is physically attractive. So, the ageing woman losing her youthful looks faces male condemnation of an inescapable process, an irony hardly ever explored in Early Modern drama. Shakespeare is the exception here, as I show in this book – particularly in my discussion of his characterisation of Cleopatra.

Not surprisingly the predominantly male-authored drama of the period also has old female characters expressing disquiet about getting on. John Marston's *The Malcontent* (1604) shows an ageing, albeit unfaithful wife, Aurelia, so deeply wounded by the reported insults of

---

6 William Brenchley Rye, ed., *England As Seen by Foreigners in the Days of Elizabeth and James the First* (New York: Benjamin Blom, 1967), 104.

7 Roy Strong, *The Cult of Elizabeth: Elizabethan Portraiture and Pageantry*, 2nd edn (London: Pimlico, 1999), 48, 50.

8 Amy Boesky, 'Giving Time to Women: The Energising Project in Early Modern England', in *'This Double Voice': Gendered Writing in Early Modern England*, ed. Danielle Clarke and Elizabeth Clarke (Basingstoke: Macmillan, 2000), 123–41 (123).

9 Ibid., 136.

her lover – he is supposed to have called her a 'dried biscuit' (1.6.18) – that she promptly replaces him to bolster her damaged self-confidence. In Webster's *The White Devil* (1612) Isabella, going into battle against a rival for her husband's affections, hopefully reminds herself that her lips are 'not yet much withered' (2.1.167).

Stereotypical ridiculing of an older woman because she is losing her looks is closely linked on stage to mockery of her sexuality. When the aged Nurse is exposed to Cupid's influence in *Dido Queen of Carthage* (1587) Marlowe and Thomas Nashe show her as a willing recipient:

> Say Dido what she will, I am not old;
> I'll be no more a widow; I am young,
> I'll have a husband, or else a lover.
> (5.1.21–3)

Cupid's disgusted response – 'A husband, and no teeth!' (5.1.24) – encourages an audience to laugh at such unseemly desires in one who is clearly past it.

Of course, there is a double standard at work with regard to sexuality in old age. In John Day's *The Isle of Gulls* (1606) the elderly Duke Basilius and his wife, Gynetia, both pursue Lisander who, disguised as an Amazon, is secretly wooing one of their daughters. Basilius is taken in by the disguise and woos Lisander as a woman, while Gynetia recognises his masculinity. The behaviour of the Duke in chasing a much younger 'female' is not questioned, while Day gets much comic mileage out of the folly of Gynetia – 'old Autumn' (5.1.G4ᵛ) – in her pursuit of Lisander. The Duke registers hypocritical disgust at her inappropriate desires – 'that a dry sapless rind / Should hold young thoughts, and a licentious mind' (5.1.HIʳ).

The sexual experience of older women, along with their being past child-bearing age and 'imagined as both lustful and undesirable', made them 'figures at the juncture of sexual anxieties' at this period.[10]

---

10 Laura Gowing, *Common Bodies, Women, Touch and Power in Seventeenth-Century England* (New Haven and London: Yale University Press, 2003), 22.

Such anxieties may account for the old woman on stage often being depicted as desperate with desire and either having to buy sex or cheat her way into bed with the male she lusts after. In *The Downfall of Robert Earl of Huntingdon* (1598) Anthony Munday and Henry Chettle show the lustful Queen Elinor disguising herself as the true object of the Earl's affections to satisfy her sexual longings:

> Now shall I have my will of Huntingdon
> Who taking me this night for Marian,
> Will hurry me away instead of her;
>
> (418–20)

Elinor fails in her attempts but another lust-driven ancient, Erictho, has better success in John Marston's *Sophonisba* (1605). Using her infernal powers Erictho disguises herself as the lovely Sophonisba and so tricks her way into Syphax's bed. Come the morning Erictho is triumphant, having satisfied her desire 'to fill / Our longing arms with Syphax' well-strung limbs' (5.1.14–15). Syphax perfectly reflects male fear and loathing here, angry less at being fooled than at being fooled into having sex with an old woman. He immediately reaches for his sword to destroy the 'rotten scum of hell' (5.1.2). Male concern about female sexuality extending into old age also fuels specific physical insults as we find in John Fletcher's *The Tamer Tamed* (1609–11). Jaques' description of one of the older women marching to support the heroine focuses with disgust on her vagina, saying this 'Looks like the straits of Gibraltar, still wider / Down to the gulf [...]' (2.3.45–6).

Along with her sagging skin, voluminous vagina and scandalous sex-drive the Early Modern stage persona of the badly behaved old woman is also easily recognised by her uncontrolled volubility, reflecting the misogynistic view of pamphleteer Joseph Swetnam that 'a woman's chief strength, is in her tongue. The serpent hath not so much venom in his tail, as she hath in her tongue'.[11] Generally, the garrulous crone

---

11 Joseph Swetnam, 'The Arraignment of Lewd, Idle, Froward, and Unconstant Women; or the Vanity of Them, Choose You Whether. With a Commendation of Wise, Virtuous, and Honest Women' (1615), in *The Whole Duty of a*

is a figure of fun like Gammer Gurton. This old woman's frenzied behaviour has house and locality in an uproar in *Gammer Gurton's Needle* (1553, published in 1575) by William Stevenson (?), particularly when she gets into a shouting match and fist fight with her equally loquacious old neighbour, Dame Chat. Similar amusement is had at the expense of the old, deaf countrywoman in *The Woman Hater* (1606) by Beaumont and Fletcher. She mishears everything and will not be silenced, as her despairing victim Gondarino confirms – 'What can she devise to say more?' (4.1.105). However, comic garrulous ramblings can also develop into dangerous speaking by older women. In Greene's *Alphonsus King of Aragon* (1587) Amurack is so incensed by his wife's refusal to be silent about his marriage plans for their daughter that he banishes the 'prattling dame', Fausta, from court and country on pain of death (3.2.1057). The Old Lady in *Henry VIII*, co-authored by Shakespeare and Fletcher, creates a risky situation through rambling repetition of Henry's dearest hopes when she presents news of Anne Boleyn's confinement to the King:

King Henry. [...] is the Queen delivered?
Say, 'Ay, and of a boy.'
Old Lady. Ay, ay, my liege,
And of a lovely boy [...]
'Tis a girl
(5.1.163–5, 166)

Inappropriate speaking in the old woman is also evidence of her potentially subversive power. Jonson's *Catiline His Conspiracy* (1611) demonstrates the dubious influence of the ageing female conspirator, Sempronia, on the married Fulvia. The older woman encourages the younger to pursue an affair, advising 'make / Use of thy youth and freshness, in the season' (2.186–7). Similar concern appeared previously in the comic piece *The Schoolhouse of Women* (1541), attributed to

Woman: Female Writers In Seventeenth-Century England, ed. Angeline Goreau (New York: The Dial Press, 1985), 69–74 (73).

Edward Gosynhill, where the older wife mischievously stirs up the younger to rebel against her husband:

> Then saith the elder, 'Do as I do;
> Be sharp and quick with him again.
> If that he chide, chide you also,
> And for one word give you him twain.'[12]

Jonson alerts us to Sempronia's essential triviality by having her reflect with surprise that 'states, and commonwealths employ not women / To be Ambassadors sometimes!' (4.715–16). This confirms her own lack of good sense rather than demonstrating a bold aspiration, for she has already shown her folly by parading her scholarship and dismissing visiting male ambassadors who do not speak Greek (4.711). So, although she boasts of her influence in helping Catiline:

> We shall make him Consul,
> [...] Crassus, I, and Caesar
> Will carry it for him.
>   (2.99–101)

and although it seems that her candidate is grateful to her, praising her remarkable powers – 'you've done most masculinely' (3.687) – it really comes as no surprise to learn that this older woman is merely tolerated 'to procure moneys' (2.194). Catiline's true feelings about her involvement in his campaign are shown in his private disgust at having to rely on the help of 'ev'n the dregs of mankind [...] whores, and women!' (3.716–17).

Uncontrolled outspokenness in an old woman at this time could also result in accusations of witchcraft. This is referred to in *The Winter's Tale* where Paulina takes pains to avoid being thought 'assisted / By wicked

---

12 Edward Gosynhill (?), 'The Schoolhouse of Women' (1541?), in *Half Humankind: Contexts and Texts of the Controversy about Women in 1580–1640*, ed. Katherine Usher Henderson and Barbara F. McManus (Chicago: University of Chicago Press, 1985), 136–55 (142).

powers' (5.3.90–91) when she undertakes the transformation of Hermione's statue. She is very much in control of this performance, as I discuss later, so the fact that she appeals for King Leontes' approval of what she will do is unexpected but also understandable, given his earlier angry references to her as 'a mankind witch' (2.3.68). His reassurances now are part of the dramatic process of healing and reconciliation but Paulina's concerns also reflect social attitudes. Although historical evidence is thin about the numbers of old women accused of witchcraft the fact of their being aged seems to have been crucial to commentators at the time. *The Discovery of Witchcraft* (1584) identifies the witch as 'commonly old, lame, blear-eyed, pale, foul, and full of wrinkles'.[13] It was doubtless 'easier to accuse those women who were more vulnerable, such as the old, widowed and poor'[14] and not surprising that 'some of the old women who were prosecuted for witchcraft were senile and of unsound mind'.[15] Clearly, Paulina is aware of the dangerous assumptions which may be made about her and moves to pre-empt these.[16]

But if witchcraft accusations are not an option there's another way of checking the old woman's runaway tongue which beleaguered male characters can use – they can dismiss her as having completely lost her marbles. In *Richard III* wrinkled Queen Margaret suffers such a fate and the effect of her prescient warnings about Richard – 'Look when he fawns, he bites;' (1.3.288) – is lost because Richard's linguistic trickery is designed to show her as slow, confused and, most repressively, 'lunatic' (1.3.277). It is telling that one of Shakespeare's more powerful

---

13 Lucy de Bruyn, *Woman and The Devil in Sixteenth-Century Literature* (Tisbury: The Compton Press, 1979), 115.

14 Marianne Hester, *Lewd Women and Wicked Witches: A Study of the Dynamics of Male Domination* (London: Routledge, 1992), 201.

15 Brian P. Levack, *The Witch-Hunt in Early Modern Europe* (London: Pearson Education, 2006), 17.

16 For more detailed work on witchcraft accusations at this time see Alan Macfarlane, *Witchcraft in Tudor and Stuart England: A Regional and Comparative Study* (London: Routledge and Kegan Paul, 1970); Frances E. Dolan, *Dangerous Familiars: Representations of Domestic Crime in England 1550–1700* (Ithaca: Cornell University Press, 1994); Marion Gibson, *Reading Witchcraft: Stories of Early English Witches* (London: Routledge, 1999).

older female characters, Volumnia the mother of Coriolanus, has a similar experience after her son's disgrace and dismissal from Rome. In Act 4 scene 2 she too becomes the butt of lunatic jibes – 'They say she's mad'; 'Why stay we to be baited / With one that wants her wits?' (*Coriolanus* 4.2.11, 18, 46–7).

Early Modern writing implies that the perfect old woman of the period is one who accepts her aged state without fuss, denies her sexuality and most importantly, provides a good example to younger women. We see the Abbess in Shakespeare's *The Comedy of Errors* (1594) take Adriana to task for jealous nagging and the young wife accepts the justice of the older woman's criticisms – 'She did betray me to my own reproof' (5.1.91). This echoes Thomas Becon's earlier stricture in *Catechism* (1564) that 'old and ancient matrons' should teach young ones to be 'sober-minded [...] discreet, chaste, housewifely; good, obedient to their husbands'.[17] Similarly, William Harrison's *The Description of England* (1587) praises the 'ancient ladies of the court' for rejecting idle behaviour in favour of such quiet occupations as reading religious texts and 'writing volumes of their own or translating of other men's into our English and Latin tongue'.[18] For Harrison the good example shown by these older women appears to be more important than the possibly challenging nature of their literary activities. The good old woman on stage guides young men as well as young women, as can be seen in *Sappho and Phao* (1584) where John Lyly gives the mature Sybilla a substantial role as advisor to Phao on the trauma of unrequited love. In Greene's *Orlando Furioso* (1591) the 'old witch', Melissa, (4.2.1236) cures the infected Orlando and sends him off to battle, earning his gratitude and his admiration of her as a 'sacred goddess' (4.2.1340).

These are general dramatic stereotypes and I will explore specific presentations of good and bad old women in Part Two of this book. Yet even in this initial overview it's clear that the 'message' from the Early Modern stage was that the old and ageing female should strive to

---

17 Thomas Becon, 'Works' (1564), in *Renaissance Women: Constructions of Femininity in England*, ed. Kate Aughterson (London: Routledge, 1995), 175–7.

18 William Harrison, *The Description of England*, ed. George S. Elden (Ithaca: Cornell University Press, 1968), 228.

---

deny her own sexuality, guard her wayward tongue and do as she was told. If not, she risked male mockery as being wrinkly, randy, mouthy and mad.

Old Women Offstage: Out and About

Historians show that during the Elizabethan and Jacobean periods most women, including those of advanced years, were active beyond the domestic sphere. While it was possible to access some charitable support – through the poor rates for example – there was no state provision of social services for the elderly. So, unless she was seriously physically disabled, retiring from work just wasn't an option for the Early Modern woman without financial independence.[19] Indeed, these old women continued to be key elements of the workforce, operating in all areas of the national economy including the cloth trade, farming, and food preparation and sale. They also worked in other retail areas, were involved in education and training, figured largely in public and private health and care work and were also active in the sex trade. In fact, 'post-menopausal women appear to have been seen as having a positive value in society which men over 50 would have lacked'.[20]

There were ageing women giving this positive value at all levels of society. Although officially excluded from involvement in politics, like their younger counterparts in Shakespeare's day, many older women operated in this arena. Queen Elizabeth, of course, was a prime example of a post-menopausal woman running a country – like her sister before her – and the women of her Privy Chamber remained in place for years. Indeed, on the accession of her husband James I to the English throne, Anne of Denmark had to institute a court shake-up and install younger women in favoured

---

19 See Sara Mendelson and Patricia Crawford, eds, *Women in Early Modern England 1550–1720* (Oxford: Clarendon Press, 1988), 281–98.

20 Margaret Pelling, 'Old Age, Poverty and Disability in Early Modern Norwich: Work, Re-marriage and Other Expedients', in *Life, Death and the Elderly: Historical Perspectives*, ed. Margaret Pelling and Richard M. Smith (London: Routledge, 1991), 74–101 (84).

court positions, preferring them to Elizabeth's ageing attendants.[21] Among Elizabeth's women who 'participated in an elaborate network of influential and political interconnection' was Blanche Parry, more than 20 years her mistress' senior.[22] Blanche is thought to have had considerable influence with the Queen, often acting as an intermediary for aristocratic appellants.[23] Throughout the period older women of the aristocracy were also active as writers, translators, and literary patrons, and examples here include Lady Anne Bacon, Mary Sidney Countess of Pembroke, and Lady Elizabeth Russell who, at 70, prepared and published her English version of a Latin work.[24] It is worth noting that often 'it was in old age, especially as grandmothers, that wealthier women enjoyed most social respect'.[25]

Positions of responsibility were held by older women in all areas of employment. Some of the matrons working at St Bartholomew's Hospital, London, were in post for long periods, including Elizabeth Collston who was matron for over 25 years.[26] A similar arrangement at Christ's Hospital saw the employment of 'a matron and twenty-five nurses' who cared for poor, orphaned children and where a nurse of 'great age' was granted a

---

21 Leeds Barroll, 'The Court of the First Stuart Queen', in *The Mental World of the Jacobean Court*, ed. Linda Levy Peck (Cambridge: Cambridge University Press, 1991), 191–208 (202).

22 Elizabeth A. Brown, '"Companion Me with My Mistress": Cleopatra, Elizabeth I, and Their Waiting Women', in *Maids and Mistresses, Cousins and Queens: Women's Alliances in Early Modern England*, ed. Susan Frye and Karen Robertson (Oxford: Oxford University Press, 1999), 131–45 (132).

23 Tracy Borman, *Elizabeth's Women: The Hidden Story of the Virgin Queen* (London: Jonathan Cape, 2009), 346. See also Charles Angell Bradford, *Blanche Parry, Queen Elizabeth's Gentlewoman* (London: R. F. Hunger, 1935); and Anne Somerset, *Ladies in Waiting: From the Tudors to the Present Day* (London: Weidenfeld and Nicholson, 1984).

24 See especially Retha M. Warnicke, *Women of the English Renaissance and Reformation* (London: Greenwood Press, 1983); and Maureen Bell, George Parfitt and Simon Shepherd, eds, *A Biographical Dictionary of English Women Writers* (London: Harvester Wheatsheaf, 1990).

25 Patricia Crawford, *Blood, Bodies and Family in Early Modern England* (Harlow: Pearson Education, 2004), 99.

26 Mendelson and Crawford, 41.

---

weekly pension and help with rent even when dismissed for negligence.[27] Mature women were also present in strength in other areas of public health and in private healing. Lady Grace Mildmay was a recognised expert in this profession, corresponding with male practitioners and exchanging findings, but there is evidence of others at all levels of society.[28] For old women the 'authority' of old age 'might be manifested in roles of caretaking, supervising, and nursing the community's bodies'.[29] Certainly such women worked in unofficial medical practice – at least 10 of 110 irregular female practitioners were described as old by the College of Physicians who were trying to control them – while among the licensed female surgeons women were still carrying out surgical procedures in old age.[30] These female professionals included 'Mother Edwin' who was paid for providing treatment at St Thomas' Hospital in 1563.[31] Old women were also employed in high-risk health work as inspectors of the living sick and the dead at times of plague outbreaks.[32]

A key figure at all levels of society was 'the woman with knowledge, the midwife who was herself a mother'.[33] The importance of the midwife is seen in the strict regulations relating to her licensing

---

27 Diane Willen, 'Women in the Public Sphere in Early Modern England: The Case of the Urban Working Poor', *Sixteenth Century Journal* 19 (1988): 559–75 (566).

28 Linda Pollock, *With Faith and Physic: The Life of a Tudor Gentlewoman Lady Grace Mildmay 1552–1620* (London: Collins and Brown, 1993).

29 Laura Gowing, *Common Bodies, Women, Touch and Power in Seventeenth-Century England* (New Haven and London: Yale University Press, 2003), 76.

30 Margaret Pelling, 'Thoroughly Resented? Older Women and the Medical Role in Early Modern London', in *Women, Science and Medicine 1500–1700: Mothers and Sisters of the Royal Society*, ed. Lynette Hunter and Sarah Hutton (Stroud: Sutton Publishing, 1997), 63–78 (72).

31 A. L. Wyman, 'The Surgeoness: The Female Practitioner of Surgery 1400–1800', *Medical History* 28 (1984): 22–41.

32 Diane Willen, 'Women in the Public Sphere in Early Modern England: the Case of the Urban Working Poor', *Sixteenth Century Journal* 19 (1988): 559–75 (572).

33 Mendelson and Crawford, 203. For details of the licensing procedures see W. S. C. Copeman, *Doctors and Disease in Tudor Times* (London: Dawson, 1960); Jean Donnison, *Midwives and Medical Men: A History of the Struggle for the Control of Childbirth* (New Barnet: Historical Publications, 1988); Jean Towler and Joan Bramall, *Midwives in History and Society* (London: Croom Helm, 1986);

through the bishops. These authorities 'were concerned chiefly with women's characters' and, of course, with their obedience to church teachings.[34] The duties of the midwife to her community might also include investigating matters such as rape, the birth of bastards and infanticide.[35] However, it was her main line of work, attending at child birth, which was likely to provide a lucrative occupation for the ageing practitioner as midwives 'could be among the better paid women workers' with particularly substantial fees going to midwives serving royalty and the aristocracy.[36] Attendance on the daughter of Sir Thomas Throckmorton was priced at a comfortable £31.[37]

Mature women also served on the Jury of Matrons which had the responsible task in civil cases of determining if a widow was pregnant by her recently deceased husband. In criminal cases the jury would examine a woman sentenced to death but pleading pregnancy and here the findings of the matrons could result in a stay of execution so this was a highly responsible task.[38]

Examples of ageing women working independently also appear in contemporary church court records. Some of them were self-supporting widows, like Elizabeth Ellell who at 50 taught 'young children to read and work with their needles' as well as working as a seamstress herself, and the 60-year-old Elizabeth Gaskyn who 'useth to keep women in childbed and [...] wash at several men's houses'. Others worked alongside their husbands like Marie Cable, aged 50, who ran her husband's butcher's shop, or in separate employment like Ann Hawes, also 50, recorded as keeping 'a sempster's shop' while her husband worked as a musician.[39]

Merry E. Weisner, 'Early Modern Midwifery: A Case Study', *International Journal of Women's Studies* 6 (1993): 26–43.

34 Mendelson and Crawford, 314.

35 David Harley, 'Historians as Demonologists: The Myth of the Midwife-Witch', *The Society for the Social History of Medicine* 20 (1990): 1–26 (10).

36 Mendelson and Crawford, 315.

37 Ibid.

38 James C. Oldham, 'On Pleading the Belly: A History of the Jury of Matrons', *Criminal Justice History* 6 (1985): 1–64.

39 Patricia Crawford and Laura Gowing, *Women's Worlds in Seventeenth-Century England* (London: Routledge, 2000), 77–80.

While some older widows would have been left destitute and reliant on support from family members or on parish charity, others enjoyed many new financial and legal benefits. Because the law could be 'time-consuming' for the widow over the claiming of her dower many such women opted for a holding in jointure lands which became theirs on the day of the husband's death, thus ensuring 'a financially secure widowhood'.[40] But whether there was a will or not the widow was legally entitled to her dower (usually a third of her husband's property) and could venture into all sorts of areas of legal process which were closed to a married woman. The widow was able to enter independently into contracts, make her own will and carry on her own business. Some widows had the important task of acting as executrix for the husband's estate and would find themselves functioning in the public world of the probate courts – 'created and maintained entirely by men'.[41] Certainly widowhood gave women access to previously forbidden areas of business. Widows of London guild members were allowed by the companies to carry on crafts and trades – 'a status unique among women in 16th century London'.[42] This also happened in York where widows of guild members were permitted to maintain family businesses as independent members and where the majority who did so appear to have functioned as 'serious and successful business women'.[43] In some cases widowed women launched financial careers, making investments and offering loans – at times relying on 'income from money lending to augment their livelihood'.[44] As well as being involved in the famous rebuilding work at the Old Hall, the widowed Bess of Hardwick used

---

40 Tim Stretton, *Women Waging Law in Elizabethan England* (Cambridge: Cambridge University Press, 1988), 27.

41 Amy Louise Erickson, *Women and Property in Early Modern England* (London: Routledge, 1993), 175.

42 Steve Rappaport, *Worlds Within Worlds: Structures of Life in Sixteenth-Century London* (Cambridge: Cambridge University Press, 1989), 40.

43 Diane Willen, 'Guildswomen in the City of York 1560–1700', *The Historian* 46 (1984): 204–18 (210).

44 B. A. Holderness, 'Widows in Pre-Industrial Society: An Essay Upon their Economic Functions', in *Land, Kinship and the Life-Cycle*, ed. Richard M. Smith (Cambridge: Cambridge University Press, 1984), 423–42 (442).

'excess revenues to offer short-term loans at good rates of interest to neighbouring landowners [...]'.[45] Other widows used their new financial powers to benefit the poor, prisons, hospitals and asylums, like Helen Branch, the widow of a former Lord Mayor of London. She also organised financial donations for the Draper's Guild and for Oxford and Cambridge universities.[46] As well as benefits like this widowhood brought responsibilities and women had to take on civic duties such as payment of taxes and parish rates, which gave them a measure of status in their community. Overall, it's not surprising that 'rich old women generally carried more clout than poor old men'.[47]

While some women working in the world of commercial sex could eventually, perhaps, achieve the status of 'rich old women' and retire comfortably, court records show that in general women too old to earn as prostitutes 'had to turn to procuring or keeping a brothel'.[48] Gilbert Dugdale's 'A True Discourse of the Practices of Elizabeth Caldwell' (1604) records the subversive behaviour of Isabel Hall, the 'ancient, motherly woman' paid by Jeffrey Bownd to procure for him a young married woman, Elizabeth Caldwell.[49] After Bownd and Caldwell became lovers – using Hall's house for their assignations – they attempted to poison Caldwell's husband with cakes laced with rats' bane, provided by Hall, and all three were eventually tried and executed. Perhaps because the two lovers were reported as making penitent ends while Hall apparently went to her death 'very stoutly denying everything' it was the older woman who drew down Dugdale's ire.[50] He labelled her

---

45 Mary S. Lovell, *Bess of Hardwick First Lady of Chatsworth 1527–1608* (London: Little, Brown, 2005), 371.

46 Joshua Sylvester, 'Monodia' (1594), in *Half Humankind: Contexts and Texts of the Controversy about Women in 1580–1640*, ed. Katherine Usher Henderson and Barbara F. McManus (Chicago: University of Chicago Press, 1985), 329–34.

47 Pat Thane, *Old Age in English History: Past Experiences, Present Issues* (Oxford: Oxford University Press, 2000), 7.

48 Mendelson and Crawford, 295.

49 Gilbert Dugdale, 'A True Discourse of the Practices of Elizabeth Caldwell', in *Writing and the English Renaissance*, ed. William Zunder and Suzanne Trill (London: Longman, 1996), 276–92 (278).

50 Ibid., 291.

the instigator 'both in the adultery and the murder' and the epitome of 'the boldness of sin'.[51]

The anonymous 'Arraignment and Burning of Margaret Ferneseede' (1608) was more explicit, describing the alleged husband-killer's progress from prostitution to becoming a bawd upon 'growing into disabled years'.[52] Remarkably, she was able to continue this trade even after marrying the respectable tailor Antony Ferneseede who was described as 'sober and of very good conversation' as compared with the 'filthily debauched' Margaret.[53] As in Dugdale's writing, there is considerable evidence of anxiety about the infiltration of respectable society by such dangerous old women. In her confession – not a first-hand testament but one written for her – Margaret Ferneseede admitted to having supplied her male customers with women she had drawn into prostitution. Some of these were wives she trapped by undermining their marriages – 'persuading them they were not beloved of their husbands' – while others were innocent young women fresh from the country. Ferneseede boasted of having 'seldom less than ten whose bodies and souls I kept in this bondage'.[54] She also confessed to receiving stolen goods but she denied killing her husband. Her conviction appeared to be based as much on her lifestyle as on the evidence of two of her 'loose customers' that heard her swear to get rid of her spouse.[55]

These images of the bawd as an old woman corrupting innocence and undermining the institution of marriage certainly match the stage representations of the character as I will show later in this book. However, research into prostitution in Elizabethan London, including into legal records, shows that women did not outnumber the men who kept brothels.[56] While the bawd was 'the chief target of the bench and

---

51 Ibid., 278, 291–2.
52 'The Arraignment and Burning of Margaret Ferneseede' in Henderson and McManus, 352–9 (357).
53 Ibid., 353.
54 Ibid., 357.
55 Ibid., 358.
56 Paul Griffiths, 'The Structure of Prostitution in Elizabethan London', *Continuity and Change* 8 (1993): 39–63.

literary invective' and always 'addressed in the feminine' pimping 'was chiefly a male task'.[57] In 1556 and 1557 Henry Machyn described the punishment of bawds in the pillory, by carting and whipping, and he identified these as male and female.[58] In the advice tract 'Look On Me London' (1613) we read of a father warning his son, who was off to sample city life, to beware of men in pubs, bowling alleys and gaming houses who would offer to 'procure a woman's acquaintance'.[59] These 'neat panders' would proceed to whisk the young innocent male off to 'some blind brothel house about the suburbs' where he could buy sex and probably contract venereal disease at the same time.[60] Clearly the corrupter of innocence imaged in this text was male.

Other tracts and sermons of the day expressed deep concern about immorality in general and prostitution in particular but condemnation of commercial sex in these works did not focus upon the female bawd. Indeed, the commonly used term 'whoremonger' usually implied a male procurer. Examples of whoremongers cited by Phillip Stubbes in *The Anatomie of Abuses* (1583) were male by a large majority. While older women were certainly involved in the organisation and provision of commercial sex, men generally maintained control of the business in a variety of roles including acting as bawds themselves and co-managing brothels. Magistrates also wielded controlling powers by imposing or withholding punishment as Stubbes, for example, was well aware. While advocating stringent methods of ridding society of prostitution he was mournfully realistic about the likelihood of disciplinary action taking place as the magistrates 'wink' at what is going on – 'They see it and will not see it' (K2ʳ). Ownership of property used for prostitution also gave men control over the trade. As Shakespeare's contemporary

---

57 Ibid., 46.
58 John Gough Nichols, ed., *The Diary of Henry Machyn Citizen and Merchant Taylor of London from AD 1550–AD 1563* (London: Camden Society, 1848), 104, 107, 161.
59 'Look On Me London – a Countryman's Counsel given to His Son Going up to Dwell at London' (1613), in *Blood and Knavery: A Collection of English Renaissance Ballads of Crime and Sin*, ed. Joseph H. Mashburn and Alec R. Velie (Cranbury, NJ: Associated University Presses, 1973), 159–75 (164).
60 Ibid., 165.

Thomas Dekker points out, the male landlord could be identified as 'the Grand-Bawd [...] sithence he takes twenty pounds rent every year [...] And that twenty pound rent, he knows must be pressed out of petticoats'.[61]

There is no personal evidence of the activities, quality of life, hopes and expectations of the bawd. Nor does the personal writing which is available offer any insight into the role and character of any particular bawds – there are no revelations about rite-of-passage brothel visits, for instance. Indeed, as this study will show, the dominant images of the bawd at this time come from the theatre of Shakespeare's day.

It's clear that in the Early Modern period older women were active and productive beyond the domestic sphere, so it's important to be aware that dramatists – Shakespeare included – do not present older women on the Elizabethan and Jacobean stage in the diverse occupations seen in contemporary life. Instead these women always appear in a family setting as ageing wives, mothers and stepmothers, widows or the family nurse. The only old woman active outdoors on stage is the bawd and even this character is seen functioning in relation to the family values which she is busy undermining. High-status old women are not immune from domestic pigeon-holing as they, too, are seen almost exclusively in relation to a husband (alive or dead) or to grown-up children. Keeping ageing and old women indoors allows for dramatic focus of course. For example, Hamlet's confrontation with his mother might carry less weight and intensity if she had vacated her closet for a site visit to her new Elsinore building project. More importantly though, placing the old woman in the home underlines the importance of family life and, as I'll show, demonstrates the perception that domesticity is a key to the successful containment of those mature women who are in danger of becoming too bold, outspoken and disobedient.

---

61 Thomas Dekker, 'English Villainies Discovered by Lantern and Candlelight' in *The Wonderful Year and Selected Writings*, ed. E. D. Pendry (London: Edward Arnold, 1969), 233–6 (233–4).

Old Women Offstage: 'Her Indoors'

Wives

However active and autonomous she might be outside the home, indoors the attitude of an Early Modern old wife was expected to match that of a younger one in terms of obedience and deference to her husband and in the performance of her domestic duties. Yet it's evident that relationships then, as now, were complex and mature couples, like newlyweds, often hit problems when aspiring to the perfect marriage.

Society in Shakespeare's day saw an interesting shift in the market for written self-help guides to marriage. Prior to the Reformation it was mainly priests who sought such advice texts, presumably so that they could provide some relevant marriage guidance to non-celibates. Gradually, though, a larger secular readership developed. Husbands and wives had greater access to lifestyle tracts on all aspects of wedlock – 'choice of partner, dominance of husband, mutual affection and respect, sexual activity, and sharing of work'.[62] Thus hopes and expectations were more widely articulated but so was the insistence, in conduct books, advice tracts and sermons, upon the subordination of the wife.[63] We even find a husband in an exceedingly elevated position, King James I, laying down the law on this matter in *Basilicon Doron* (1599 – reprinted upon his accession to the throne in 1603). The married monarch insisted that a husband rule his wife as a 'pupil' and that there should be restrictions upon her learning – 'teach her not to be curious in things that belongeth her not [...] It is your office to command, and hers to obey' (O1^r–O2^v).[64] Wifely disobedience would only lead to disorder, as William Whately pointed out in his *A Bride Bush* (1617). Warning 'Out of place, out of peace', he stated that it was a

---

62 Kathleen M. Davies, 'Continuity and Change in Literary Advice on Marriage' in *Marriage and Society: Studies in the Social History of Marriage*, ed. R. B. Outhwaite (London: Europa, 1981), 56–80 (78).

63 This area of publication is explored in depth in *Chaste, Silent and Obedient: English Books for Women 1475–1640*, ed. Suzanne Hull (San Marino: Huntington Library, 1962).

64 James I, *Basilicon Doron (1599)* (Menston: The Scolar Press, 1969).

wife's duty 'to acknowledge her inferiority'.[65] That such subordination must continue throughout a marriage was emphasised in 'An Homily Against Excess of Apparel', one of those read out in churches throughout Elizabeth's reign and attributed to Bishop Pilkington. He cited St Peter on how properly 'the old ancient holy women attired themselves, and were obedient to their husbands'.[66] Outside the conduct book genre emphasis was also placed upon a woman bowing to her husband's wishes. 'A Wife' (1614) – attached to the *Overburian Characters* – focused upon a woman's essential readiness to be moulded to her husband's needs, 'For when by Marriage both in one concur, / Woman converts to Man, not Man to Her'.[67] This was very much in line with the sentiments expressed in 'A Good Woman' – 'her chiefest virtue is a good husband. For She is He'.[68]

Our knowledge of women's hopes and expectations for marriage is limited, but the letters of Joan and Maria Thynne reveal a big difference between women's actual experiences and what they were encouraged to expect of husbands, as set out in the very advice tracts designed to guide their own behaviour. Joan Thynne disliked her husband's absences, expecting a husband to 'share a wife's company – a factor stressed in the texts', while Maria demanded her rights of household management – 'if she recognized his sphere in the outside world [she] was entitled to her say indoors'.[69] These two wives objected to the fact that they didn't experience the 'ideal of manhood derived from the prescriptive texts'.[70] The Thynnes weren't alone in experiencing such dissatisfaction. The majority of wives who sought the help of seventeenth-century astrologer and physician, Richard Napier, were distressed 'because they

65 William Whately, 'A Bride Bush' (1617) in *Renaissance Women: Constructions of Femininity in England*, ed. Kate Aughterson (London: Routledge, 1995), 33.

66 John Griffiths, ed., *The Two Books of Homilies Appointed to be Read in the Churches* (Oxford: Oxford University Press, 1859), 316.

67 Sir Thomas Overbury (?), 'A Wife' (1614), in *The Overburian Characters to Which Is Added A Wife*, ed. W. J. Paylor (Oxford: Basil Blackwell, 1936), 108.

68 Paylor, ed., 'A Good Woman', 4.

69 Alison Wall, 'Elizabethan Precept and Feminine Practice: The Thynne Family of Longleat', *History* 75 (1990): 23–38 (29).

70 Ibid., 30.

expected to be treated fairly and affectionately' in their marriages and were disappointed.[71]

But it would be wrong to assume that all marriages were under strain and there are glimpses of comfortable marital relationships at this time with wives enjoying strong and lasting bonds with their husbands. The correspondence between Lord Arthur Lisle and his wife Honor shows great affection on both sides indicating a companionable partnership.[72] A caring relationship between Margaret Countess of Lennox and her husband is also suggested in the concern she expressed when writing to Sir William Cecil in 1569 – 'it toucheth me nearest to see my L. my husband who and I have been together this xxvi years, fall into such an extreme heaviness'. She and Lennox were eager to gain guardianship of their grandson, the young James I, but although this is a politically-motivated letter the concern the Countess has for her husband is apparent as she frets over being unable 'by any mean to comfort him'.[73] Lady Grace Mildmay's collection of meditations (though not written for publication) shows that she too felt partnership should exist in a good marriage. While wives ought to 'submit themselves unto their husbands as unto the Lord [...] as the church is in subjection unto Christ', husbands are urged to 'love your wives even as Christ loved the church and gave himself for it'.[74] Though their marriage wasn't an easy one Grace Mildmay and her husband seemed to have achieved mutual affection in their relationship. Of course, it may have helped that she maintained a career of her own – her medical activities which 'were practised on a large, expensive and systematic scale'.[75] The intellectual and creative satisfaction gained here may well have mitigated any sense of irritation about subjection to a husband's rule.

---

71 Michael Macdonald, *Mystical Bedlam: Madness, Anxiety and Healing in Seventeenth-Century England* (Cambridge: Cambridge University Press, 1981), 102.

72 Muriel St Clare Byrne, ed., *The Lisle Letters*, vol. 1 (Chicago: University of Chicago Press, 1981).

73 Henry Ellis, ed., *Ellis's Original Letters*, 2nd series (London: Harding and Leopard, 1827), 333.

74 Linda Pollock, *With Faith and Physic: The Life of a Tudor Gentlewoman Lady Grace Mildmay 1552–1620* (London: Collins and Brown, 1993), 44.

75 Ibid., 44.

The firmest evidence of mutual trust in marital partnerships is apparent with wives acting publicly on behalf of their husbands. Lady Katherine Paston dealt with suits in Chancery for her husband Edmund while he was 'exceeding sickly'; she wrote letters, conducted all arrangements and made all the necessary decisions. In her copious correspondence to her son, William, who was at Cambridge, Lady Katherine also relayed messages and gifts from her husband, maintaining crucial family connections.[76]

However, when marital troubles arose these often centred on lack of wifely obedience. George Carew's letters to Sir Thomas Roe provided gossipy details of a major 'domestic' between Sir Edward Coke and his wife Elizabeth in which the subordinate role was thoroughly flouted. Lady Elizabeth objected violently to the proposed marriage of their youngest daughter, to the extent that she tried to gain custody of the daughter 'by force'.[77] Here the disobedient wife found herself at odds with her monarch, James I, as well as her husband as the potential bridegroom was a member of the favoured Villiers family. The betrothal and eventual marriage did take place but while Lady Elizabeth was absent, 'under restraint', obviously continuing to defy both patriarchs with remarkable boldness. Such insubordination in a wife was worrying for those men involved and for those observing. Coke experienced the personal discomfort of his position at court being affected by Elizabeth's bad behaviour and Carew's correspondence did not omit the pleasing conclusion – 'Within two or three days following Sir Edward Coke was restored again to his place in the Counsel'.[78] John Smyth, recording the lives of the Berkeley family, showed similar unease about the behaviour of Anne Savage, second wife of Thomas, Lord Berkeley, 'a lady of masculine spirit, over-powerful with

76 Ruth Hughey, ed., 'Lady Katherine Paston to Francis Bacon, Lord Verulam, 29 April, 1619', 'Lady Katherine Paston to William Paston, January 1624, June 1624', in *The Correspondence of Lady Katherine Paston 1602–1627* (Norfolk: The Norfolk Recording Society, 1941), 51, 65–6, 72.

77 John Maclean, ed., *Letters from George Lord Carew to Sir Thomas Roe Ambassador to the Court of the Great Mogul 1615–1617* (London: The Camden Society, 1860), 119.

78 Ibid., 120

her husband'. Smyth's concern was also provoked by Anne's daughter-in-law, Katherine who, in her 'middle and elder years', always wanted to know what her husband was doing and the details of his financial dealings. Smyth commented disapprovingly, 'For the most part it falleth out that where wives will rule all they mar all'.[79]

The emphasis upon expected perfection in a wife indicates considerable male anxiety about potential imperfections – disobedience, disloyalty and disorderly behaviour. As I show in this book these issues are highlighted in mature marriages in the drama of the period.

Mothers

Given the caring, nourishing and guiding behaviour implicit in being a good mother it's not surprising that, although Elizabeth I had no offspring of her own, she happily acknowledged the image of herself as virgin mother to her people presented in public writings of the period.[80] Indeed, this was reinforced by Elizabeth's godson, John Harington, who wrote to his wife of, 'Our dear Queen [...] and this state's natural mother [...]'.[81] The importance of motherhood and of positive maternal influence was emphasised in contemporary writings and while there was no specific advice material for the mature mother there were dire warnings of how the spoiling of a son or sons could rebound upon a woman in later life. In the *Overburian Characters* – 'Her Next Part' – the young mother bequeaths her unpleasant qualities to her eldest son, guiding his education in entirely the wrong direction – 'her utmost drift is to turn him fool'.[82] The result appears in the character

---

79 John Maclean, ed., *The Berkeley Manuscripts: The Lives of the Berkeleys by John Smyth of Nibley*, vol. 2 (Gloucester: Bristol and Gloucestershire Archaeological Society, 1933), 263, 387.

80 Lena Cowen Orlin, 'The Fictional Families of Elizabeth I', in *Political Rhetoric, Power and Renaissance Women*, ed. Carole Levin and Patricia A. Sullivan (Albany: State University of New York Press, 1995), 81–100.

81 Leanda de Lisle, *After Elizabeth: How James King of Scots Won the Crown of England in 1603* (London: Harper Collins, 2005), 10.

82 Paylor, ed., 5.

'A Golden Asse' where the son, when an adult, suffers the results of that early influence – 'he is as blind as his mother, and swallows flatterers for friends'.[83] Two cautionary tales from Thomas Beard also show the long-term effects of early spoiling. He cites a Flanders mother who lavished money on her two sons in their youth, 'against her husband's will', only to be racked with guilt when, as grown men, the pair fall 'from rioting to robbing' (O4ᵛ). Her conscience 'told her that her indulgence was the chiefest cause' says Beard (O4ᵛ). Beard also describes another mature mother who has her ear bitten off by her son who, about to be hanged, blames her for not chastising him more often in his youth (O4ᵛ).

Personal writing of the time shows that older mothers continued to be closely engaged with the lives of their adult sons. For example, Lady Anne Bacon, mother of Antony and Francis, wrote to them in 1590 giving unsolicited advice on everything from etiquette – 'courtesy is necessary, but too common familiarity in talking and words is very unprofitable' – to their everyday lifestyle – 'I pray you be careful to keep good diet and order'. She urged them not to let their men drink wine in hot weather, not to loan out their own transport to others, and to get to bed earlier. Her tart reflection, 'my sons haste not to hearken to their mother's good counsel' indicates that the Bacon brothers did not spring into corrective action on receipt of her letters of guidance.[84] However, her interest and interference in their lives seemed to spark no ill-feeling in her offspring. A letter from Francis to his mother in 1594 urged her to look after herself in turn – 'use all the comforts and helps that are good for your health and strength'.[85] Lady Katherine Paston also showed close maternal concern for the health and welfare of her student son, urging upon him good behaviour and habits of hard work and politeness to his teachers. William was instructed not to eat too much fruit, to use liquorice rather than tobacco and to avoid 'possetty curdy drinks' which his mother believed to be 'most unwholesome and very clogging to the stomach'. Like the Bacons, William seemed to take

---

83 Ibid., 7.

84 James Spedding, ed., *The Letters and Life of Francis Bacon*, vol. 4 (London: Longmans, Green, Reader and Dyer, 1868), 113–15.

85 Ibid., 300.

this fussing in his stride, writing back fondly. His mother was delighted by his reassurance that he liked to hear from her often.[86]

While a mother could use her position to attempt to influence and persuade on her son's behalf this had to be done with delicacy. When the son of Anne, Duchess of Somerset was banged up in the Tower – after secretly marrying Lady Catherine Grey, one of Queen Elizabeth's potential heirs – this anxious mother sought the help of Sir William Cecil and the Earl of Leicester. In a carefully worded letter the Duchess suggested that if the two took up her cause, pressing for the release of her son, 'the more shall you set forth the Queen's Majesty's honour; and as a mother I must needs say, the better discharge your callings and credits'.[87] This reference to her own position carried an image, albeit obliquely presented, of the approval of the mothers of the powerful men whose support she needed. However, where a mature mother stepped beyond the bounds of appropriate behaviour it was clear that she couldn't rely on maternal privilege for a defence, as Lady Lennox found after organising the marriage of her son to another claimant to the English throne. Her excuse was that of the doting mother whose son had 'entangled himself so that he could have none other' so that she simply had to promote the marriage, 'he being mine only son and comfort that is left to me'.[88] Queen Elizabeth ignored such maternal excuses, however, and imprisoned Lady Lennox for her political impudence.

A son as 'comfort' to an ageing mother was of practical as well as emotional importance. If that mother was widowed or poor, a good relationship with a son could mean the difference between a comfortable and an uncomfortable old age. Strong ties would also benefit the mother's own social position and enhance her influence. The mother of George Villiers was active in bringing her son to the notice of King James and when he became the monarch's favourite, and she the Countess of Buckingham, her power increased.[89]

---

86 Hughey, ed., 72, 78.
87 Ellis, ed., 287.
88 Ibid., 323–4.
89 Edward Phillips Statham, ed., *A Jacobean Letter-Writer: The Life and Times of John Chamberlain* (London: Kegan Paul, Trench, Trubner, 1921), 179–80.

Older mothers would be expected to guide daughters as well as sons, focusing on obedience to the appropriate dominant male (father, husband or prospective husband) and emphasising the duties and responsibilities to be taken on with marriage. It is interesting to note that in reality such obedient behaviour was neither enacted nor advocated by Margaret, Countess of Cumberland, who challenged her husband's will on behalf of her daughter, Lady Anne Clifford. This resulted in much legal wrangling as well as marital tussles for Anne but she expressed no criticism of her mother's actions and example, and when the Countess died Anne described the loss as 'the greatest and most lamentable cross that could have befallen me'.[90]

And it wasn't unusual for a mother to intervene in her adult daughter's life in the delicate area of marital conflict, where issues of female obedience could be openly challenged. Church records reveal that mothers attended court to speak out for daughters against abusive husbands.[91] This kind of maternal support is also seen in Lady Anne Stanhope's letters to Sir William Cecil in 1569 on behalf of her daughter whose husband had thrown her out, installing 'a naughty pack' in her place. She begged Cecil to use his influence with the erring husband to get her daughter re-admitted into the marital home. However, a mother had to take care not to challenge the status quo with regard to marriage. While, with practical good sense, she urged that if mediation failed Cecil try and 'order it so that she may, having some allowance, live with her friends', Lady Anne did not support a separation. Instead she reassured Cecil, 'I will do the part of a mother to frame her to devise by all good and godly means possible to recover him to that contentation which should be their greatest comfort'.[92]

Stepmothers

In many families the early death of the mother, a mother's illness, or the separation of parents resulted in children being cared for by

---

90 H. Clifford, ed., *The Diaries of Anne Clifford* (Stroud: Allan Sutton, 1990), 36.

91 Sara Mendelson and Patricia Crawford, eds, *Women in Early Modern England 1550–1720* (Oxford: Clarendon Press, 1988), 160–61.

92 Ellis, ed., 322.

a grandmother who would often take over responsibility for their education.[93] The death of the mother, though, would usually be followed by remarriage of the father, bringing a stepmother into the domestic circle. Contemporary sources have few examples of bad stepmothers. In *The Theatre of God's Judgements* (1597) Thomas Beard made a tremendous to-do about the prevalence of the wicked stepmother and the 'many horrible murders' (S6^v) such women have committed with their stepchildren as victims. He came up with little hard evidence, however. According to Beard such domestic carnage was carried out either to enable the stepmother's own offspring to usurp the inheritance of her stepchildren or simply to wreak a nasty revenge. He boasted of knowing of 'many hundred' such incidents but in fact offered only two irrelevant examples of the bloodthirsty stepmother (S7^r). Beard's polemic is well weighted with evidence of other forms of wickedness, from disobedient children to thieves and robbers – taking in the deleterious effect of 'plays and comedies' en route (Aa7^r). So it's strange that where the wicked stepmother is concerned he leaves further research, somewhat vaguely, to the 'judgement and reading of the learned' (S7^r).

Detailed work on the Havering community does reveal wills in which the husband insisted that his children by his first marriage be supported by their stepmother after his death, which suggests a need to ensure this would happen. One William Hampshire 'made arrangements before his death in 1598 in case his second wife and older son were unable to live together'.[94] Yet while this evidence indicates that conflict could exist we also find striking images of stepmothers acting positively in the affairs of their extended families. One of Lady Anne Bacon's stepsons commented

---

93 See for example Kenneth Charlton, 'Mothers as Educative Agents in Pre-Industrial England', *History of Education* 23 (1994): 129–56; and Caroline Bowden 'Commentary on Rachael Fane, Page of Her School Notebook' in *Reading Early Modern Women: An Anthology of Texts in Manuscript and Print 1550–1700*, ed. Helen Ostovich and Elizabeth Sauer, assisted by Melissa Smith (London: Routledge, 2004), 75–7.

94 Marjorie Keniston McIntosh, *A Community Transformed: The Manor and Liberty of Havering 1500–1620* (Cambridge: Cambridge University Press, 1991), 50.

on her 'goodwill' in helping with the education of his young wife.[95] Bess of Hardwick 'was an indulgent and even affectionate stepmother' referring to the daughters of her second husband, Sir William Cavendish, as her own.[96] Later in life she was a friend to Gilbert Talbot the son of her fourth husband, George Talbot Earl of Shrewsbury, after a major falling out between father and son – supporting him 'when the old Earl had refused to do so'.[97]

Because 'step parents were inevitably common, as remarriages were frequent' the role was doubtless a tricky one for men as well as women and the general lack of public discussion of the wicked stepmother stereotype could indicate that male writers did not care to open up an area so universally problematic.[98]

Widows

When exploring contemporary attitudes towards widows, we find much evidence of male concern and confusion. Ideally the widow should be devastated and inconsolable. However, it is seen as equally important for the widow to remarry and once again place herself under the guidance of a man – and this applies particularly to the widow who is left financially independent by her husband's death. There was 'considerable anxiety [...] as to what use widows will make of their freedom from the rule of husbands'.[99]

Male-authored writing on widowhood at this time presented it as an unpleasant state – not, primarily, because of the dreadful grief and loneliness but because the widow, lacking the guiding hand of a husband, was likely to become badly behaved and at the same time

95 Lisa Jardine and Alan Stewart, *Hostage to Fortune: The Troubled Life of Francis Bacon* (London: Victor Gollantz, 1998), 33.
96 Lovell, 60.
97 Ibid., 371.
98 D. M. Palliser, *The Age of Elizabeth: England Under the Later Tudors 1547–1603* (London: Longman, 1992), 54.
99 Ruth Kelso, *Doctrine for the Lady of the Renaissance* (Urbana: University of Ilinois Press, 1956), 131.

sexually rapacious. Robert Burton pictured the ageing widow as 'unseemly' in her eagerness to remarry, to 'have a stallion, a champion' despite being 'so old a crone, a beldame'.[100] This is much in line with the misogyny of Joseph Swetnam (1615) for whom widows were 'the sum of the seven deadly sins, the Fiends of Satan, and the gates of Hell'. Most worrying was the wealthy widow – 'if she be rich, she will look to govern [...] commonly widows are so froward, so waspish and so stubborn thou canst not wrest them from their wills'.[101] The idea of a woman who cannot be controlled is very alarming and Swetnam emphasises the fact that it is possession of wealth which empowers the widow in this worrying way.

Male concerns were also engaged by the widow's opportunity to construct exclusive networks, often with her own kind – for widows didn't automatically make their homes with their offspring – '[i]t is not true that the elderly and the widowed ordinarily had their married children living with them'.[102] Investigation of Cambridge households reveals 'how rare it was for a widowed person to join the household of one of their married children'[103] while the diaries and writings of Stuart women show that wealthy widows were able to achieve supportive and powerful matriarchies. It seems that even poor widows might create some kind of community.[104]

100 Robert Burton, 'The Anatomy of Melancholy' (1621), in *The Anatomy of Melancholy*, vol. 3, ed. Thomas C. Faulkner, Nicolas K. Kiessling and Rhonda L. Blair (Oxford: Clarendon Press, 1994), 56.
101 Joseph Swetnam, 'The Bearbaiting or the Vanity of Widows, Choose you Whether' in 'The Arraignment of Lewd, Idle, Froward and Unconstant Women' (1615), in *Half Humankind: Contexts and Texts of the Controversy about Women in 1580–1640*, ed. Katherine Usher Henderson and Barbara F. McManus (Chicago: University of Chicago Press, 1985), 190–216 (216, 214).
102 Peter Laslett, *The World We Have Lost: Further Explored* (London: Methuen, 1983), 91.
103 Nigel Goose, 'Household Size and Structure in Early Stuart Cambridge', in *The Tudor and Stuart Town: A Reader in English Urban History*, ed. Jonathan Barry (London: Longman, 1990), 117.
104 Sara Heller Mendelson, 'Stuart Women's Diaries and Occasional Memoirs', in Prior, 180–210 (198–9).

It's also important to be aware that then, as now, not all women were able to marry or, indeed, chose to do so. Often, though, they are counted in the same category as widows and the experiences of the latter taken 'as representative of both groups of women' leaving 'the unique experiences of never-married women unexamined'.[105] However, there is evidence to show that menopause and old age may have 'signalled a rise in autonomy' for the single woman, 'thus allowing her to live more independently'.[106]

Nurses

There is no advice literature on the employment of a mature carer for adolescent girls and this very gap suggests that the wet nurse might remain employed by the family to become, in turn, dry nurse and old nurse, as her charge or charges grew. Close consideration of paintings in the genre of 'the doctor's visit' directs attention to a possible contemporary image of the nurse, as such pictures feature a girl, who may be lovesick, attended by an older woman in the presence of the doctor. A trusting relationship between ageing attendant and young woman is suggested by 'the knowingness of the old woman, based on her experience and familiarity with the girl's body, which is crucial for the observer'.[107] However, these are stock characters of this type of picture, so the placing of the old woman might be more significant in terms of contrasting knowledgeable age and inexperienced youth, rather than as a definite portrait of a nurse. Personal writing of the Early Modern period does not engage with this character – there are no recollections about the old family nurse, just as there is nothing about the bawd. Here we'll see that the stage persona of the older

---

105 Amy M. Froide, *Never Married Singlewomen in Early Modern England* (Oxford: Oxford University Press, 2005), 15.

106 Ibid., 23.

107 Margaret Pelling, 'Thoroughly Resented? Older Women and the Medical Role in Early Modern London', in *Women, Science and Medicine 1500–1700: Mothers and Sisters of the Royal Society*, ed. Lynette Hunter and Sarah Hutton (Stroud: Sutton Publishing, 1997), 66.

nurse provides imaginative detail to counteract lack of contemporary information about this woman and her position in the family and it is telling that, on stage in Shakespeare's day, the images of old nurse and old bawd mirror one another.

Clearly there were many valuable roles for Early Modern old women, belying their limited dramatic presentation as wife, mother, stepmother, widow, or as a nurse or bawd. It is interesting though, that even this domestic containment does not seem sufficient and that dramatic stereotyping also highlights with distaste her loss of looks, with derision her supposed sexual rapacity and with anxiety her uncontrolled outspokenness. Literary images were valuable to men in this respect, helping establish 'control of women through their fear of fitting an absurd or dishonourable stereotype'.[108] But such uses can be counter-productive. Regularly reassured that she is falling short of male standards because she is past her best, a woman can cease to value or care about such male judgements. So the situation which threatens the old woman can, paradoxically, empower her. As we shall see, it is this empowerment which Shakespeare emphasises and celebrates.

108 Joy Wiltenberg, *Disorderly Women and Female Power in the Street Literature of Early Modern England and Germany* (Charlottesville: University Press of Virginia, 1992), 253.

Part II

DRAMATIC STEREOTYPES OF THE OLD WOMAN

Loyal and Loving

The ageing female characters – wives, mothers, widows and nurses – discussed in this section express love and loyalty to those they are close to and are mainly stereotypical in their observance of deferential behaviour to their menfolk. The exceptions are the character of Isabella in Webster's *The White Devil*, loyal wife of the adulterous Duke Bracciano, and the Countess Roussillion, mother and surrogate mother in Shakespeare's *All's Well That Ends Well* (1606–1607). I discuss these characters in greater detail, showing that they are presented with a certain amount of depth and complexity, moving tantalisingly beyond the stereotypes without actually subverting them.

That loyalty to a husband is expected even when he is patently undeserving is highlighted in John Fletcher's *The Tragedy of Valentinian* (c.1614) and *The Honest Lawyer* (1615) by S. S. Valentinian is acknowledged as 'a bad man [...] a beast' (5.2.61) who dies a particularly nasty if well-deserved death. However, although his most recent infidelity has involved the very public pursuit of a friend's wife and her eventual rape, Valentinian's ageing spouse Eudoxa – her face 'Long since bequeathed to wrinkles' (5.6.9) – remains loyal to her dead husband, referring to him as her 'noble lord' (5.8.96). She marries his killer then poisons her new spouse at a celebratory banquet. Threatened with instant death by the men about her for the heinous offence of husband-murder, Eudoxa convinces her hearers that she has dispatched a traitor and is finally confirmed as 'virtuous' (5.8.1124). In *The Honest Lawyer* the long-suffering wife of Vaster selflessly offers to 'work or beg' (1.A4ʳ) for her obsessively jealous husband when he seemingly falls on hard times.

To test her loyalty he sells her to a brothel, fakes his own death and subjects her to further rejection and humiliation before their eventual and remarkable reconciliation. The example offered in these cases is clear enough: duty to a husband is paramount.

I've noted the importance of ageing mothers providing on-going guidance as well as love for their offspring and there are two early examples of this in John Phillip's *The Play of Patient Grissil* (1559) and *Appius and Virginia* (1563) by R. B. In these plays the old women are both near death and vanish from the stage early on, so their most significant action is passing on the right sort of advice on female obedience. Grissil learns from her mother that 'many words' in a young woman 'is unfit' (315) and that she should 'grudge not in ought' to her father (318) while Mater urges Virginia to 'be constant' to her husband and 'Love, live and like him well' (1.79–80). Appropriate mothering is also seen in Greene's *Alphonsus, King of Aragon* (1587) and *John a Kent and John a Cumber* (1589) by Anthony Munday, where mothers who initially support their daughters' opposition to arranged marriages eventually bow to expedience and advise these daughters to do the same. Similarly, Lady Capulet in Shakespeare's *Romeo and Juliet* (1595) shows a correct example to a daughter resisting her father's plans. However, her disregard for her daughter's feelings is clearly callous – 'I would the fool were married to her grave' (3.5.140) – so, while maternal firmness can be applauded, maternal unkindness in forcing a daughter to marry against her will is made more problematic on stage. In Fletcher's *The Night Walker* (1611) the Lady attempts a forced marriage for her daughter and in this instance it is the Nurse who takes her mistress to task over the choice of husband:

> **Nurse.**   Well Madam, well, you might ha chose another.
>   A handsomer for her years.
> **Lady.**   Peace he is rich Nurse,
>   He is rich and that's beauty.
> **Nurse.**   I am sure he is rotten,
>   Would he had been hang'd when he first saw her.
>   (1.3.12–17)

Such criticism from a paid servant, coupled with the Lady's somewhat discomfited response – 'Termagant! What an angry quean is this!' (1.3.16) – suggests that the nurse occupies a position in the family where her caring views carry some weight.

Maternal concern for preserving her daughter's chastity prior to marriage is also seen as crucial. In Greene's *James IV* (1590) the monarch's extra-marital pursuit of Ida is frustrated by that young woman's modest good sense, inculcated by her mother. Indeed, the Countess of Arran warns that this is the case when seeing off the King's go-between, 'Good sir, my daughter learns this rule of me / To shun resort and strangers' company' (2.178–9). Widow Capilet, in Shakespeare's *All's Well That Ends Well*, is equally concerned for her daughter's chastity, supporting the young woman's rejection of Bertram in spite of their having fallen into poverty. The Widow agrees to help Helena, who is married to Bertram, to bring off the bed-trick only when convinced it will not result 'in any staining act' (3.7.6–7).

On stage a mother's participation in a married daughter's affairs is imaged as praiseworthy only if correct. Mistress Touchstone in *Eastward Ho!* (1605), by Chapman, Jonson and Marston, initially attracts disapproval by supporting the extravagances of her wealth-obsessed and status-seeking daughter, Gertrude. However, when the young woman's new husband loses all their money Mistress Touchstone adopts a much more appropriate maternal stance by trying to instil proper behaviour into her daughter, who now needs all the family support she can get – 'Speak to your father, Madam, and kneel down [...] O Madam, why do you provoke your / Father thus?' (4.2.132, 182–3). Although she's a comic figure Mistress Touchstone expresses a mother's responsibilities in continuing to school a daughter in difficulties. The importance of perpetual guidance of this kind can excuse apparent acts of defiance by mother and daughter. In *The Triumph of Love*, one of *Four Plays or Moral Representations In One* (1612) by Fletcher, Beaumont and Field (?), Angelina cares for her daughter Violanta, who has given birth after secretly marrying the man she loves against paternal wishes.

New motherhood reminds Violanta of all that her mother has done for her:

> **Violanta.** Alas, dear mother, you groaned thus for me,
> And yet how disobedient have I been?
> **Angelina.** Peace, Violanta, thou hast always been
> Gentle and good.
>
> (3.100–103)

The fact that they are complicit in defying the wishes of husband and father is offset by Violanta's newly-achieved penitence and appreciation of suitable female conduct, confirmed by her mother's tender silencing of her. Therefore, the play's happy ending can be seen as appropriate.

The stereotypically good mother will also demonstrate care of her son or sons by working on their behalf. In Shakespeare's *Cymbeline* (1610–11) the imprisoned and entirely downcast Posthumus is lucky enough to have his mother return from the dead, with other deceased family members, to plead with Jupiter on his behalf (Act 5 scene 5). The thoroughly alive and strong-minded Agrippina, in Jonson's *Sejanus His Fall* (1603), is equally caring of her sons and tries to inspire their resistance to Sejanus:

> Then stand upright
> And though you do not act, yet suffer nobly:
> Be worthy of my womb and take strong cheer.
>
> (4.73–5)

Though Sejanus prevails his description of how he has dealt with the threat – 'set my axe so strong, so deep / Into the roots of spreading Agrippina' (5.249–50) – engages with a matriarch whose actions on behalf of her sons command respect, even if she is an enemy. William Rowley's *A Shoe-Maker A Gentleman* (1608) also reveals a powerful mother taking control of her sons' actions at a time of crisis. Eldred and Offa are determined to avenge their dead father while their mother wants them safe in hiding until resistance stands a better chance. It is interesting to note that in this play the Queen uses an important inducement, a mother's blessing, to bring about her sons' agreement – 'I'll take my blessing off if you delay / And plant my curse instead' (1.B3ʳ). The blessing and the curse of a good mother, representing parental approval or disapproval, could be used powerfully by dramatists to establish audience response to the offspring concerned. Eldred and Offa immediately obey their mother, disguise themselves and take up humble employment. As good sons and therefore good men they are seen to deserve happiness at the play's conclusion. However, in *Richard III* Richard seeks the blessing of his mother only to mock it:

> 'And make me die a good old man.'
> That is the butt-end of a mother's blessing;
> I marvel that her grace did leave it out.
>
> (2.2.97–9)

We're hardly surprised when the Duchess later presents this bad son with a catalogue of his sins and delivers herself of a 'most heavy curse' (4.4.188). Throughout this confrontation Richard behaves in a thoroughly shifty fashion, trying to deflect his mother's attack with feeble jokes and eventually acknowledging his discomfort, 'You speak too bitterly' (4.4.181). The Duchess concludes her curse by negating maternal support – 'My prayers on the adverse party fight' – and uttering a grim prophecy – 'Bloody thou art, bloody will be thy end' (4.4.191, 195). She exits without Richard making any response. Although this mother cannot influence alteration in her son's behaviour Shakespeare shows that her complete division from him is enough to silence the usually articulate Richard. Their total separation comes to mind again in Act 5 when the challenger, Richmond, refers before battle to his own 'loving mother' and is assured of her blessing (5.5.35–6).

While drama of the period often images love between mother and daughter this is never elevated to the almost reverential attitude seen in some stereotypical mother-son relationships. In Kyd's *The Spanish Tragedy* (1587), for example, Isabella experiences a vision of her murdered son, Horatio, seated Christ-like in heaven, supported and uplifted by cherubim, with his wounds 'newly-healed' (3.8.19). It comes as no shock that Isabella goes mad with grief and frustration over the lack of justice for this seemingly sanctified son. Veneration of a similar fervour grips Elinor, the Queen Mother in Peele's *Edward I* (1591). Her eagerness to be reunited with her 'lovely Edward' is not deemed foolish – ''tis but mothers love' – even when she faints away at the sight of her boy (1.29.A2^v, 1.44.A3^r). In Henry Chettle's *The Tragedy of Hoffman* (1602) we see the Duchess Martha prepared to wait all night 'on the humble earth' (4.2.1715) for the arrival of her son and when she falls asleep at this task she presents an image of 'one of her sex so perfect' that the vengeful Hoffman is unable to kill her (4.2.1864). When she learns that her son is dead she wants only to entomb herself in a cell with his body.

But, while a measure of self-denial on a son's behalf is deemed admirable, dramatists are wary of presenting a positive view of maternal sacrifice if this undermines moral principles. In Middleton's *No Wit No Help Like a Woman's* (1613) Lady Twilight lies about her chastity at her son's request in order to protect him yet this is not seen as admirable self-sacrifice but the cause of further conflict. Tamora in Shakespeare's *Titus Andronicus* (1592) is imaged as bad throughout the play, though her actions are rooted in the desire to avenge the death of one of her sons. Her protestations of maternal love cannot justify her subsequent actions, which include instigating the rape and mutilation of Titus's daughter Lavinia. Similarly, the Queen in *Cymbeline*, planning to poison both her husband and her stepdaughter, cannot possibly be considered a good mother even though her motive is the advancement of her son Cloten.

Exceptions to this condemnation of mother as avenging tigress appear in Chettle's *The Tragedy of Hoffman* and in Beaumont and Fletcher's *A King and No King* (1611). The Duchess Martha using her feminine attractions to lure Hoffman to his death is justified dramatically by his being a 'cruel murderer' who has killed her son (5.3.2575). But we see that, although devious in her entrapment of Hoffman, Martha otherwise maintains her purity and goodness throughout the play – unlike Tamora and *Cymbeline*'s Queen, who are morally flawed. The image of Arane, the Queen Mother in *A King and No King*, is more complicated. She is initially perceived as a wicked mother determined to kill her son, Arbaces, but is finally revealed as a good mother, planning the murder simply for the benefit of her daughter, the true monarch. The problem is solved by the revelation that Arbaces is not Arane's son; yet the happy ending, with the King who is no king marrying the newly-discovered Queen, leaves an uncomfortable understanding that this mother's attempts at murder, to gain her daughter's rights, have been acceptable because the person she has tried to kill is not a blood relative!

It is relevant that reconciliation between a mother and her offspring at the conclusion of a play can signify a setting aside of conflict and herald new beginnings. The Abbess in Shakespeare's *The Comedy of Errors* describes her years of separation from her twin sons in terms of a lengthy labour 'and till this present hour / My heavy burden ne'er delivered' (5.1.404–5) and so the reunion is imaged as a new birth, a fresh start. In *Pericles* (1607) and *The Winter's Tale* (1610) the mothers embrace and bless their newly found daughters, adding religious emphasis to the sense of renewal with which each play closes.

Webster, in *The White Devil*, gives us an exciting glimpse of a tough-minded, ageing woman who challenges the idea of marital obedience and discovers an empowering way of coping with her husband's betrayal of her love and trust. Isabella is sometimes presented as a pious, virtuous wife (in pallid contrast to her rival for her husband's affections, the wicked, vigorous Vittoria). But although Isabella even takes responsibility for her separation from Bracciano, apparently turning the other cheek in a move of fine Christian martyrdom, she is far from being a doormat. I think it important to be alert to the influence of her age on her behaviour – she is hurt and embittered at being rejected for a younger woman: 'Are all these ruins of my former beauty / Laid out for a whore's triumph?' (2.1.238–9). Webster shows us a loving and loyal mature wife who knows her husband well and at first firmly believes she can win him back. That she understands him is obvious from the way she warns her brother Francisco that applying a 'rough tongue' (2.1.11) is not the way to handle Bracciano. She briskly announces that she forgives her husband – 'all my wrongs / Are freely pardoned' (2.1.12–13) – and then reassures Francisco that she knows exactly how to resolve the problem:

> [...] these arms
> Shall charm his poison, force it to obeying
> And keep him chaste from an infected straying.
> (2.1.16–18)

She is sure she can heal Bracciano and physically reclaim him with the force of her love-making and realises only gradually that she has badly misread the situation. When she and Bracciano meet her manner is open and friendly, not hesitant or self-deprecating and even when he accuses her of jealousy she responds wittily – 'I am to learn what that Italian means' (2.1.161). But when her husband refuses to kiss her and avoids her embrace in a way that emphasises physical distaste – 'O your breath!' (2.1.163) – her self-confidence is shattered as seen from her anxious reference to her age and loss of looks:

> You have oft for these two lips
> Neglected cassia or the natural sweets
> Of the spring violet, they are not yet much withered,
> (2.1. 165–7)

Now her wit forsakes her and Bracciano takes the chance to put Isabella in the wrong by taunting her as a stereotypically disloyal and disorderly ageing wife. He claims she has complained about him to her family and chased after other men (2.1.172–7). Small wonder that she briefly wishes she were dead (2.1.178–9) and in her 'winding sheet' (2.1.205). The extreme nature of her reaction implies that such cruelty from Bracciano isn't a typical experience for her. It's only when he announces that he won't sleep with her again that Isabella pulls herself together, challenging his denial of 'the sweet union / Of all things blessed' (2.1.198–9). She loves this man and wants to share his bed, convinced that this is where she has the best chance of reclaiming him. When he proves adamant in rejecting her she insists on becoming 'the author' of his decision (2.1.218) taking control of the situation, of her own life and to a certain extent of her husband. For, while she may forfeit family and public respect by seeming to instigate their separation, she binds her husband to her in a different way, as only he knows the truth about their deal. In the scene they play out for Francisco's benefit, Isabella's is the central role while Bracciano cuts a sorry figure with his feeble protestation 'You see 'tis not my seeking' (2.1.265). Isabella turns all her husband's earlier cruelty against him with wonderful irony, kissing him to seal their separation and repeating his own word 'never' (2.1.254) to confirm her decision.

In engaging so closely with an older woman who challenges the stereotypical good wife mould while functioning within it Webster engages briefly with an intriguing character – loyal to her husband, doing her best to get him back and, in failing, refusing to give up without a fight – before he focuses full dramatic attention on her competitor. It is telling that Isabella's murder takes place as a dumb show. We do not hear that passionate and sympathetic voice again.

Shakespeare does not subvert the stereotype of the good old woman as mother in *All's Well That Ends Well* but, like Webster with Isabella, he approaches the role in a way which challenges expectations. The Countess sets her son, Bertram, an example of behaviour by compartmentalising her expressions of affection into what is appropriate for the public and private spheres of life. Unlike standard doting mothers she is uncomfortable with showing maternal affection for Bertram, yet is able to relate generously to the surrogate daughter, Helena. Her behaviour raises questions about her attitude to self-presentation, public and private, and shows that her own confusion about this may have influenced Bertram's immaturity. It is evident that correct behaviour is very important to the Countess. We see this in her comments on the way Helena conducts herself (1.1.45–8) and in her advice to the young woman against overdoing mourning – 'No more of this, Helen. Go to, no more' (1.1.48–9). Even on greater issues she is most concerned with social propriety. When she hears that Bertram, now married to Helena, has abandoned his new wife the Countess is as horrified by his discourtesy to the King, who promoted their marriage, as by his dishonouring of the young woman (3.2.28–32). When Helena returns after this incident, clearly distraught, the Countess urges her to be calm – to behave properly – giving herself as an example:

> Think upon patience [...]
> I have felt so many quirks of joy and grief
> That the first face of neither on the start
> Can woman me unto't
>
> (3.2.48–51)

Her concern with Helena's conduct is expressed in the context of her care of and affection for the young woman and this closeness is reflected in the way she re-lives her own youth through Helena's passion for Bertram – 'Even so it was with me when I was young' (1.3.124).

Yet Shakespeare shows that the Countess is unable to achieve such warmth with her son and while she admits affection for Bertram she cannot do so to his face. In the opening scene of the play, when Bertram leaves for Court, the Countess expresses her feelings formally and obliquely – 'In delivering my son from me, I bury a second husband' (1.1.1–2). Although the final lines of the Countess' farewell blessing reveal some anxiety for her son this is couched in terms of his possibly lacking guidance and does not articulate motherly affection – 'good my lord, / Advise him' (1.1.68–79). Her emphasis is on correct behaviour as she urges him, Polonius-like, to 'Love all, trust a few, / Do wrong to none' (1.1.61–2).[1] Only when alone can the Countess reveal the depths of her affection for her son and even then this is linked to her love for Helena:

> which of them both
> Is dearest to me I have no skill in sense
> To make distinction.
>
> (3.4.38–40)

---

1 See William Shakespeare, *Hamlet*, in John Jowett, William Montgomery, Gary Taylor and Stanley Wells, eds, *The Oxford Shakespeare: The Complete Works*, 2nd edn (Oxford: Clarendon Press, 2006), 1.3.58–77

Bertram's equally formal farewell to his mother contains no loving words but focuses upon his own bereavement (1.1.3–4). Clearly his attitude is influenced by hers and since mother and son both mention the loss of husband and father at parting it could be that this dictates the way they now relate to each other. Shakespeare goes no further into this but his expression of the Countess' self-restraint in connection with Bertram, set against her lively and relaxed exchanges with Lavatch, her Clown, and her overt care for Helena, hints at the complex and uneasy relationship between mature mother and adult son which the playwright explores in much more depth in *Coriolanus* and *Hamlet*.

Embarrassing and Bawdy

Although she is not necessarily imaged as a bad old woman, the mature mother who causes embarrassment for her offspring is often a comic stage stereotype. That the offspring concerned is always a son touches on adult male anxieties over unsuitable maternal manners but in the majority of these situations the son concerned is far from being an admirable person himself. So humour is to be had at the expense of both embarrassing mother and squirming son as my examples here will show.

In Middleton's *Michaelmas Term* (1606) poverty-stricken Mother Gruel arrives in London seeking her son Andrew, who has changed his name to Lethe and is aspiring to high status and a wealthy marriage. She doesn't even recognise her smartened-up offspring and when she talks to this 'stranger', seeking information, Mother Gruel comically reveals enough of his background and true nature to make him thoroughly uncomfortable and so delight the audience:

> I have known the day when nobody
> cared to speak to him [...]
> His virtues? No, 'tis well known his father was too
> poor a man to bring him up to any virtues [...]
> he has no good parts about him.
> (1.1.274–5, 280–82, 285–6)

In an attempt to secure this loose cannon of a mother the still unrecognised son employs her to carry messages to his prospective bride but Mother Gruel embarrasses him further by delivering the subsequent rude rejection to Lethe in front of the very friends he wants to impress. Middleton also adds an interesting edge when Lethe, faced with punishment at the end of the play unless he can get someone to speak on his behalf, turns to his mother sure that she will help him. Realising now that her cheapskate employer is her 'wicked son Andrew' (5.3.155) Mother Gruel takes her revenge. She delivers a brisk sermon on how he has changed – 'when thou had'st scarce a shirt, thou had'st / More truth about thee' (5.3.161–3) – and then falls tantalisingly silent. The play ends with neither audience nor Lethe knowing if she will eventually plead for him.

Embarrassment is the only form of punishment facing Abraham, in Nathan Field's *A Woman is a Weather-Cocke* (1609). His mother, Lady Ninnie, shames him with her drunken and incontinent habits – 'I have seen her so bepiss the rushes as she has danc'd / at a wedding' (3.2.25–6). However, he is an unpleasant young man and gains no sympathy here. Again, when the horrid Tim returns from Cambridge in *A Chaste Maid In Cheapside* his doting mother feeds him plums 'like a child' (3.2.155), forces him to kiss her female friends and reveals his adolescent failings to his tutor. 'These women must have all out' Tim complains (4.1.63) but he clearly deserves such a mother.

It is interesting to note that in Middleton's *The Witch* (1615) even Hecate, the most powerful and unpleasant of witches who merrily boils up unbaptized infants, is mocked behind her back by her son, Firestone. While she dotes on him he merely wants her out of the way, describing his mother, with her companion witches, as 'foul sluts' (3.17). His reason for disliking Hecate has to do with her power, which he doesn't share. As she flies up to join her spirits he sulks below, 'Well mother, I thank your kindness: you must be gambolling i' the air, and leave me to walk here like a fool and a mortal' (3.81–3). The resentment of this son of a witch who cannot attain his mother's superior power is comparable to that of mortal progeny who are equally aware of the potent 'magic' any mother has to turn her adult offspring into a cringing child once more with an embarrassing word or action.

Bawdy language and behaviour are not the prerogative of the old woman on stage but playwrights certainly access these attributes in their characterisations of the old nurse and old bawd. Both women are presented as garrulous, outspoken, salacious and lust-driven – all recognisable aspects of the stereotypical ageing female. It is often through linguistic confusion that nurse and bawd will demonstrate their seeming stupidity and become figures of fun on stage. In Marston's *The Dutch Courtesan* (1604) Nurse Putifer unconsciously presents a double meaning when boasting of her dancing skills – 'my traverse forward, and my falling back' (3.1.194–5) – and this confirms her as a daft old dame. The same play finds the old bawd, Mary Faugh, blamed by the prostitute, Franceschina, for the girl's downfall. The old bawd responds with outraged and outrageous protests of good faith – 'I could not ha' sold your maidenhead oft'ner than I ha' done!' (2.2.10–12).

Both characters are irrepressibly verbose and outspoken. Juliet's talkative Nurse rattles on mindlessly when arranging the tryst between her charge and Romeo – 'What wilt thou tell her, Nurse? Thou dost not mark me' (2.3.165–6) – and in Jonson's *Cynthia's Revels* (1601) we see Madam Moria ridiculed by Cupid as 'A lady made all of voice and air, talks anything of anything' (2.3.14–15). However, comic clack is also seen as a worrying trait. Juliet's nurse warns Romeo 'if you should deal double with her, truly it were an ill thing to be offered to any gentlewoman, and very weak dealing' (2.3.158–60) but then is too busy chattering to check the young man's response. Madam Moria fantasises about learning all the secrets of the court:

> I would tell
> you which madam loved a monsieur, which a player,
> which a page; who slept with her husband, who with her friend
> [...] who with her monkey
>
> (3.1.152–6)

and does not seem aware of the threat in Phantaste's response – 'Fie, you'd tell all, Moria. If I should wish / now, it should be to have your tongue out' (3.1.158–9). So the verbosity of nurse and bawd, like that of all old women, is allowed as comic and entertaining but is also seen as problematic because the speaker lacks self-control.

As well as this shared garrulousness there is frequent deliberate use of vulgar jokes, *double entendres* and sexual imagery in the language of both women. A fine example is the coarseness of Juliet's nurse in re-telling an old joke – 'dost fall upon thy face? / Thou wilt fall backward when thou hast more wit' (1.3.41–2) – and her, perhaps unwittingly, lewd encouragement of the downcast Romeo, 'Stand, and thou be a man / [...] rise and stand!' (3.3.87–8). In contrast we find the seeming subtlety of the bawd Sweatman in Cooke's *Greene's Tu Quoque or The City Gallant* (1611) who complains that her 'forepart [...] is worn so bare' (4.357) during a discussion which is apparently about gowns. Of course the nurse and the bawd are not the only stage characters to speak in this way and provide comedy through sexual innuendo but their use of such language generally has deliberate titillation as a common purpose. The nurse will use it to spark off her charge's interest in marriage and also to excite the male suitor; the bawd to maintain the interest of her male clients and to persuade any woman she is procuring of the pleasures to be found in the arms of the pursuer. Such language can also provide titillation for an audience, of course. This shared purpose, along with the language itself, also ties these old women together in terms of status on stage, traditionally placing both at the lower end of the social scale.

Alongside such comic images we often find a further powerful, dramatic presentation of bawd and nurse as being especially dangerous to other, younger women. Here shared characteristics in both women include greed and underhand dealing, as the older woman supplements her earnings with extra gifts from males desiring access to the young woman in her charge or over whom she has influence. Nurses like Juliet's, though modestly refusing payment for their 'pains' (2.3.172) have it thrust upon them anyway. Others, less fastidious, take the tips without fuss, as in Marston's *Antonio's Revenge* (1600) where Piero, wooing the widowed Maria, works successfully through her nurse and servant, as we see in the 'dumb show' at the start of Act 3 – *Piero bribes Nutriche and Lucio; they go to her, seeming to solicit his suit.*

Deception is part and parcel of the modus operandi of the bawd. For example, Birdlime, in Dekker and Webster's *Westward Ho!* (1604), provides services for the three city wives while secretly juggling their husbands in and out of the bed of her most popular prostitute. Yet the nurse, too, is often cunning and treacherous, despite her being in a position of trust – close to her charge and an influence upon her. Indeed, if she had been her charge's early wet-nurse the bond would be doubly powerful.[2] We see aspects of this in a number of plays. In *Romeo and Juliet* the privileged involvement of Juliet's Nurse when Lady Capulet decides to test the water regarding a match for her daughter is a clear mark of family trust. Initially barred from this 'counsel' (1.3.10) the Nurse is hastily co-opted and allowed to contribute, albeit bawdily, throughout the *tête-à-tête* between mother and daughter.

But rather than use her position to restrain her charge the nurse will often connive with, and even encourage, disobedience of parental ruling by the girl for whom she is responsible. For example, in Samuel Daniel's *Hymen's Triumph* (1614) the nurse, Lydia, encourages her charge to lie about her pursuit of a young man. Deception may be in the cause of true love and may result in a happy-ever-after ending with the parents finally accepting their daughter's choice, but it's clear that the nurse's actions are not what an employer would wish in a paid and trusted servant. More importantly, they can result in disaster for the young woman concerned. Juliet's Nurse betrays family trust in actively supporting her charge's relationship with Romeo: even after the killing of Mercutio she helps the lovers consummate their secret marriage. And in an interesting extension to this nurse's deceit Shakespeare shows her urging Juliet to cut her losses, once Romeo is banished, and marry Paris who is the parental choice. Perhaps the Nurse truly believes that Juliet's

---

2 See Diana E. Henderson, 'The Theatre and Domestic Culture', in *A New History of Early English Drama*, ed. John D. Cox and David Scott Kaston (New York: Columbia University Press, 1997), 173–94.

first marriage is as good as dead and that a second will not be bigamous, or perhaps she belatedly realises where her family loyalties should lie. At all events she attempts to stimulate Juliet's enthusiasm with romantic images of Paris:

> An eagle, madam,
> Hath not so green, so quick, so fair an eye
> As Paris hath.
>
> (3.5.219–21)

This ironically harks back to, and falls short of, the language she used previously in promoting Romeo's charms – 'and for a hand and a foot and a body, though they are not / to be talked on, yet they are past compare' (2.4.41–2).

Like the Nurse, the stage bawd can aid and abet women eager for sexual adventure. These are not the prostitutes under her charge in the brothel but women like the wife of Elbow the constable in *Measure for Measure* (1603–1604). She has been a regular visitor to the Overdone establishment as the interrogation of Pompey reveals:

Escalus. Now, sir, come on.
What was done to Elbow's wife, once more?
Pompey. Once, sir? There was nothing done to her once.
(2.1.133–5)

Similarly, the wives in *Westward Ho!* use the bawd, Birdlime, to cover their tracks when planning an outing with three young gallants and when the wives are shopped to their husbands it's Birdlime who rushes off to warn them. However, her intervention proves unnecessary as these canny women are well able to extricate themselves from the clutches of their companions and an awkward situation.

While providing services for such wives appears to be a sideline to Birdlime's main line of work the bawd Maquerelle in *The Malcontent* has the unfaithful Duchess Aurelia as her prime client. However, we see here that a bawd's essential greed and cunning can render her untrustworthy when Maquerelle proves herself a useless look-out by allowing the Duchess to be caught *in flagrante* – 'I, like an arrant beast, lay in the outward chamber, heard nothing' (4.2.19–20). There is a similar moment in *The Dumb Knight* (1608) by Gervase Markham and Lewis Machin, which emphasises this worrying carelessness in the bawd. Collaquintida stands helplessly by when the husband of her client, Lollia, arrives home early while the unfaithful wife is entertaining the lover:

> **Lollia.**　　　　O Mistress Collaquintida, what shall
> 　　　　　　　become of us?
> **Collaquintida.**　Nay, I'm at my wit's end and am made
> 　　　　　　　Duller than any spur-gall'd, tired jade.
> 　　　　　　　　　　　　　　(3.1.F2ᵛ)

It's some fast footwork by Lollia which eventually saves the day, but Duchess Aurelia is not so lucky, even though she defends herself when discovered. It's amusing and ironic that Maquerelle goes on to piously refer to the Duchess' experience as an example when advising other women of the court – 'O beauties […] Be sure the door be bolted' (4.1.22–3).

Another major stage activity for the bawd is to procure honest young women for dishonest men and we see Maquerelle engaged in this, later in *The Malcontent*, when she is hired to tempt the virtuous Maria. A bawd's skill in this area is often demonstrated by reference to her already having drawn a number of young women into her trade and playwrights surround the bawd with an atmosphere of sleaze and corruption and show her as a thorough-going danger to other women. Yet the bawd is often unable to entrap the honest and innocent woman and Maquerelle's failure with Maria is not untypical in dramatic terms. Attempting to persuade the young woman to submit to the desires of another man, Maquerelle cynically attacks Maria's character – 'she was a cold creature ever… she had almost brought bed-pressing out / of fashion' (5.2.84, 89–90) – and dismisses her loyalty, 'what's constancy, but fables feigned, odd old / fools chat, devised by jealous fools to wrong our liberty?' (5.3.13–14) However, she cannot prevail. Similarly, Birdlime in *Westward Ho!* is unable to procure the wife of Justiniano for the lustful Earl, even though Mistress Justiniano has been deserted by her unpleasant husband and is well aware of how difficult life will be on her own. Birdlime focuses on the lonely woman's fears, offering a common-sense solution: Mistress Justiniano should make use of her 'commodity of beauty' (2.2.186) while she can. But this wife has a strong will – 'Witch, thus I break thy spells: were I kept brave / On a King's cost, I am but a King's slave' (2.2.197–8) – and is able to walk away from temptation. Even though Birdlime, Maquerelle and their like may not prove a great deal of use to their predatory male clients this is not meant to detract from the threat they pose to innocent women. Nor does it undermine the sense of satisfaction, within the play, when their blandishments are rejected.

When innocence is overcome, despite resistance, blame also focuses on the bawd, even though she may not be the immediate agent of the young woman's downfall. The happily married Lucina, in Fletcher's *The Tragedy of Valentinian*, is beset by two court procurers, Ardelia and Phorba, who are paid to entice her into the Emperor's bed. They use familiar techniques: mocking Lucina's 'idol, honour' (1.2.1) and urging the young matron to maximise her assets – 'all that blessed beauty / Kept from the eyes that make it so, is nothing' (1.2.15–16). They also offer her jewels. But they add an intriguing spin to their procuring by suggesting that as Valentinian's mistress Lucina can become a power to do her country good – 'if anything redeem the Emperor / From his wild, flying courses, this is she [...]' (1.2.66–7). In this play, though, the honest woman is not able to walk away from the threat against her. Lucina is tricked by Valentinian into going to court and there she is raped by him. Where Ardelia and Phorba fail in their psychological entrapment the man in the case succeeds by use of brute force.

The image of the struggle of youthful female innocence against ageing female corruption carries much dramatic impact in these plays. A powerful example also appears in Shakespeare's *Pericles* where Marina, trapped in a brothel, will not be 'bowed' (4.2.83) and ignores the Bawd's hopeful instructions, 'You must seem to do that fearfully which you commit willingly' (4.2.111–20). Marina is subverting best practice for prostitutes as the outraged Bawd discovers – '[…] she would make a puritan of the devil if he should cheapen a kiss of her' (4.6.10). Marina's goodness overcomes the lust of both the high-status Lysimachus and the pimp Boult, but we are diverted from the exploitative roles these men play in the brothel by the callous wickedness of the Bawd. Deciding that rape is the only way to bring the evangelical innocent into line she chillingly orders the pimp, 'Use her at thy pleasure. Crack / The glass of her virginity, and make the rest malleable' (4.6.139–41).

In *A Mad World My Masters* Middleton allows the bawd's actions and behaviour to reveal the effects of the precarious world of commercial sex upon those who must make their living in it. In prostituting her daughter the Courtesan, the Mother has a clear agenda to benefit them both. She will achieve the financial security which, by implication, she has previously enjoyed – 'The sums that I have told upon thy pillow! / I shall once see those golden days again' (1.1.150–51) – as a result of the young woman using her wiles to entice a rich fool into marriage. The bawd is aware that such a marriage is the only way for her daughter to achieve 'the opinion for a virtuous name' (1.1.164) but calculates that once she is settled in this respectable state her daughter 'May sin at pleasure, and ne'er think of shame' (1.2.165). This cynical image of married life reflects the way in which women become commodities in the world of commercial sex and how they can sometimes work the system to their own advantage. The Mother is a stereotypical bawd. When she identifies Follywit as the fool whose inheritance will ease their existence she uses standard tricks to catch him, talking up the Courtesan's 'bashful spirit' and offering her as an enticing 'foolish virgin' (4.5.30, 36). Yet within the stereotype we glimpse the greater complexity of a woman striving to move her daughter out of the dog-eat-dog world in which they live. Clearly it's becoming harder to keep ahead of the game, as the Mother reflects:

> The shallow ploughman can distinguish now
> 'Twixt simple truth and a dissembling brow.
> Your base mechanic fellow can spy out
> A weakness in a lord, and learns to flout.
>
> (1.1.139–42)

So, once Follywit is trapped into marrying the Courtesan, Mother and daughter unblushingly weigh up the young woman's options for continuing her career:

Mother. Who covets fruits, ne'er cares from whence it fell;
Thou'st wedded youth and strength, and wealth will fall.
Last, thou'rt made honest.
Courtesan. And that's worth 'em all.

(4.5.134–7)

When these old women are brought to book it is the bawd who most regularly receives public punishment on stage, while the nurse's actions are rarely condemned in public. Often the old nurse will disappear from the action well before the play's end and is not mentioned again, though this doesn't necessarily imply that she goes unpunished for any wrong-doing. Dramatists of the period may simply be reflecting the fact that the head of a family would deal privately with an erring employee for 'servants were legally considered dependent on their employers and could be punished or dismissed by them with little recourse'.[3] In the same way, the stage bawd's public punishment could also reflect the social regularisation deemed necessary at the time. Because the bawd operates in the public sphere she cannot be dealt with in private and social order is only seen to be restored when those in power publicly allocate punishment to her. It is unusual to find a bawd rewarded as in Thomas Heywood's *The Wise Woman of Hoxton* (1604), when the old woman is given pride of place at the happy-ever-after weddings which conclude the play. Generally, bawds are imprisoned, like Shakespeare's Mistress Quickly and Mistress Overdone, though in *Valentinian* Fletcher images a kind of natural justice when the old women who tried to entrap Lucina are murdered by 'the women of the town' (5.2.58). However, he doesn't indicate whether those administering punishment are honest women or disgruntled madams. Generally the punishment meted out to

---

3 Merry, E. Weisner, *Women and Gender in Early Modern Europe* (Cambridge: Cambridge University Press, 2000), 114.

the bawd brings about her squeals of protest to add comedy to the final scenes of many a play. However, in *A Warning For Fair Women* (1599) the bawd Anne Drury is unusually shown in a state of repentance – 'My soul was ignorant, blind and almost choked / With this world's vanities' (21.2635–6) – and there is an assumption of eventual redemption – 'I am as well resolved to go to death / As if I were invited to a banquet' (21.2637–8). This conclusion for the character is linked with the real events from which the play is adapted – the murder of George Sanders by the man who seduced Sanders' wife with Drury's help. Like other bawds Drury also boasts of how easily she will achieve Anne Sanders' capitulation – 'she shall have much ado / To hold her own when I begin to woo' (1.1.314–15). Here, though, the evil influence of the bawd turns the situation from seduction into husband-murder so, although it is Browne who carries out the killing and brings down the law on all concerned, use of the stereotype demands that considerable blame focus on Drury.

This divergence with regard to punishment marks the only substantial difference between the characters of nurse and bawd in their stereotypical presentation on stage. While the stage nurse is part of the domestic structure and the bawd functions in the uncertain world of commercial sex, a world supposedly far beyond and inimical to the family structure, the stage representations of these characters are remarkably similar. There is also a distinct crossing of the line between bawd and nurse in Shakespeare's Mistress Quickly, a bawd in both parts of *Henry IV* and in *Henry V* but reinvented in a rather more respectable persona in *The Merry Wives of Windsor*. Despite having 'ministered to Prince Hal's wants' Mistress Quickly and Doll her prostitute 'remain legal and social castoffs' and are duly punished by their illustrious client.[4] In *The Merry Wives of Windsor*, however, Mistress Quickly is revived as housekeeper to Dr Caius – 'in the manner of his nurse' (1.2.3) – and in this social position becomes the accepted confidante of Mistress Ford and Mistress Page and a nurse figure to Anne Page (2.1.149–55). This shift is not entirely inappropriate to the character. In her appearances

---

4 Anne M. Haselkorn, *Prostitution in Elizabethan and Jacobean Comedy* (Troy: The Whitston Publishing Company, 1983), 47.

in *Henry IV 1 and 2* Mistress Quickly is 'constantly asserting her own respectability' and is eager to rise above her position, which makes her an easy target for Falstaff who promises marriage while robbing her blind.[5] Her nurse-like role in *The Merry Wives of Windsor* is an ideal transformation and Shakespeare uses the similarity of the stereotypes to show how little adaptation is needed.

When Quickly and Falstaff are reunited he makes use of her again in a bawd-like capacity, to act as messenger to and from the wives and to procure these women for him. Another aspect of the bawd stereotype is referenced here, for the honest and faithful wives are more than a match for her. At the same time the nurse-like Quickly is approached by the various suitors of Anne Page and encouraged to promote their cause. Stereotypically she bemoans her torn loyalties – 'I would my master had Mistress Anne; or... Master Slender... or, in sooth, I would Master Fenton had her. / I will do what I can for them all three' (3.4.101–5). However, she acts 'speciously for Master Fenton' (3.4.106) who has given her a cash bribe and who she finds the most attractive – 'A woman would run through fire and water for such a kind heart' (3.4.101–2).

There are references here, then, to the deceitful nurse involved in subverting parental wishes and the deceitful bawd, out to entrap honest women but failing to do so. There is comedy drawn from the nurse/bawd stereotype in Mistress Quickly's bawdy innuendo and in her making a fool of herself linguistically, applying a coarse reading to schoolboy Latin:

Evans.	What is your genitive case plural, William? [...]
William.	*Genitivo: horum, harum, horum.*
Mistress Quickly.	Vengeance of Jenny's case! Fie upon her! Never name her, child, if she be a whore.

(4.1.52, 55–7)

---

5 Jyotsna Singh, 'The Interventions of History', in *The Weyward Sisters: Shakespeare and Feminist Politics*, by Dympna Callaghan, Lorraine Helms and Jyotsna Singh, (Oxford: Blackwell, 1994), 7–58 (36).

So, although Mistress Quickly appears to have crossed over into respectability, from bawd to nurse, Shakespeare makes use of the similarities between these stereotyped characters to show the equivocal nature of this transformation. It is not so much that Mistress Quickly's old habits have died hard but that she and the dramatist can utilise them again in her new capacity. In a play supposedly designed as a vehicle for the resurrected Falstaff the reanimation and doubtful alteration of the one-time bawd provides parallel comedy to the portrait of a man who has not changed at all.

Disobedient and Dangerous

In Early Modern writings a woman's obedience to the dominant male in her life was presented as ideal behaviour whatever the woman's age. With stereotypical characterisations of older women much of the drama of the day emphasised the dangers of disobedience and here we find that Shakespeare's work is no exception. Of course women behaving badly are much more engaging characters for playwrights and audiences alike which was one reason for their predominance. However, it's interesting to note just how many older women were shown as disobedient and in need of masculine schooling. This surely reflected considerable male concerns about such women flouting family rules but also, reassuringly, demonstrated many methods of containing and constraining the insubordinate senior.

The importance of a husband continuing to exercise control over his ageing wife is most remarkably represented in Marston's *Antonio's Revenge* (1600). In this version of the *Hamlet* story the hero's mother, Maria, is preparing, albeit unwittingly, to wed the very man who murdered her husband. And she is duly admonished: not by her son but by the ghost of her dead spouse. Andrugio, perched on his wife's bed the night before the nuptials, first reads her a lecture on marital fidelity beyond the grave – 'Hast thou so soon forgot Andrugio? / Are our love-bands so quickly cancelled?' (3.5.3–4) – but then he forgives her and urges her to join their son, Antonio, in his plan for revenge. Antonio arrives rather late on the scene, ready to harass Maria, but it is her husband who is in control here. Even without having both feet in the grave a strong husband can redeem an errant wife, as we see in John Lyly's *Endymion* (1588). The disgraced and ageing sorceress, Dipsas, is offered forgiveness as long as she renounces her 'horrible and hateful trade' (5.4.274) and is reconciled to her husband, Geron. Geron's generous reception of his estranged wife – 'with more joy than I did the first day' – is seen as part of Dipsas' salvation and she promises to confess to him 'the cause of these my first follies' (5.4.278).

A husband's inability to control his wife often becomes the stuff of stage comedy, especially when wifely wilfulness leads to public wrangling. In Shakespeare's *Richard II* (1595) the Duke of York determines to reveal the treachery of his son to the new monarch but his disobedient Duchess refuses to obey her husband's edict. When the Duke has an audience with King Henry, the couple's private bickering threatens to spill over into the royal presence. However Henry defuses the tension by identifying that the Duchess' intervention – shouting for entry and pleading 'Speak with me, pity me! Open the door!' – shifts the situation 'from a serious thing' (5.3.72, 77). A potentially problematic scene is turned to comedy and the cause of the dispute resolved with a display of regally paternalistic mercy. Similarly, in George Chapman's *An Humorous Day's Mirth* (1597) Countess Moren's public nagging of her husband, which embarrasses him and his friends, is silenced by the King. Seemingly, neither of these husbands has the authority of Simon Eyre, in Dekker's *The Shoemaker's Holiday* (1599), in dealing with an outspoken wife. He puts his sharp-tongued spouse Margery firmly in her place – 'quarrel not with me and my men [...] Away, rubbish. Vanish, melt, melt like kitchen stuff!' (7.43, 51).

If a wife is not kept in line by a husband's firm governance her bad behaviour may extend beyond disobedience, as in Shakespeare's *Pericles* (1607). Dionyza's calm assumption of her ability to control her husband Cleon – 'But yet I know you'll do as I advise' (17.52) – shows exactly where this relationship has gone wrong. Without her husband's firm hand Dionyza has become a 'harpy' of a wife, planning the murder of Pericles' daughter Marina, who has been left in her care, and calmly dismissing her husband's pangs of conscience (17.47).

It's telling that Dionyza's 'envy' and 'vile thoughts' are damned by another male, Gower (15.37, 41). It is sometimes the case on the Early Modern stage that when a husband fails to school his wife the task can be taken on by another strong male character. At the end of the play Gower informs us that Dionyza and Cleon have been burned to death in a local uprising sparked off by leaked information about 'their cursed deed' (22. 119). This seems somewhat harsh, given that the cursed deed was not actually carried out but it's clear that Cleon's responsibility for his wife's wicked ways requires that he share her punishment.

In Chapman's *The Blind Beggar of Alexandria* (1596) Queen Aegiale who rules her husband, Ptolemy, also turns out to be a treacherous adulteress. Ptolemy's collusion in her disobedience is made obvious when Aegiale is allowed to publicly criticise him for what she decries as his weak handling of their daughter's reluctance to marry – 'You take a course my Lord to make her coy' (4.15). She compounds this by her interference in offering lengthy advice to her would-be son-in-law. Chapman embellishes this stereotypical treatment of the undisciplined Aegiale by emphasising her sexual desires. She admits that her passion for another man is out of control, picturing herself as a tireless sexual predator – 'like an Eagle prying for her prey' – in her search for him (1.58). That a wife who exerts power over her husband will incline to promiscuity is also imaged in George Peele's *Edward I* (1591) where Elinor, who easily overrules her husband the King, reveals that she has been unfaithful with his brother and that all her children are illegitimate.

There is an intensely focused examination of the marital difficulties of mature couples in Henry Porter's *The Two Angry Women of Abingdon* (1588) but though this highlights disobedient wives there is also criticism of the husbands whose behaviour fuels their defiance. The play charts the breakdown of neighbourly relations between Mistress Barnes and Mistress Goursey, a situation which turns very nasty indeed when marriage between their offspring Mall Barnes and Frank Goursey is projected. From the outset Porter's two angry women are established as disorderly refusing, in company and with much ill will, to do as their husbands ask. At a local gathering which rapidly turns sour Mistress Goursey sits down to cards with Mistress Barnes and says she will play 'A pound a game' (1.1.93).

Her horrified husband attempts to dissuade her, urging economy, but she is tartly defiant – 'No, we'll be ill housewives once: / You have been oft ill husbands – let's alone' (1.1. 97–8). Soon after this Mistress Barnes, who believes that her husband has been unfaithful with Mistress Goursey, sets up a vicious exchange of sexual *double entendre* over the card table. Barnes tries to curb her and gets short shrift:

Barnes. Go to – be ruled, be ruled!
Mistress Barnes. God's Lord! be ruled, be ruled!
What, think ye I have such a baby's wit
To have a rod's correction for my tongue?
(1.1.180–83)

This disorderly indiscipline in the wives continues throughout the play until their somewhat unbelievable reconciliation in Act 5. Like other dramatists of the period Porter emphasises that it is weakness in a husband which can allow a wife to develop such rebellious ways. This is seen in particular with Goursey who sets a bad example in the home by explaining to his son how easy and pleasant it is to stray after marriage (3.2. 109–17). It is hardly surprising, therefore, that when he tries to conceal a letter his wife snatches it, provoking an unseemly struggle, verging on a fight, refusing all the while to be overborne by him – 'I will not be afraid at your great looks' (3.3. 218).

Mistress Barnes' inability to make peace with her husband is rooted in her knowledge that she is ageing and her suspicion that he has been unfaithful. There is a deftly handled scene between the couple in which Porter shows the husband's initial attempts to soothe and encourage his wife undermined by his unwitting revelation that her bad temper is destroying her charms:

O, do not set the organ of thy voice
On such a grunting key of discontent.
Do not deform the beauty of thy tongue
With such misshapen answers
(2.1.480–83)

Small wonder that her tight response is 'So, have ye done?' (2.1.489) and that a full-scale row ensues. Her obvious reasons for opposing her daughter's marriage to the son of her enemy are augmented by a jealousy of Mall which is rooted in age difference and sexual envy. She dismisses Mall as too young to marry and when her daughter counters with the obvious question about her mother's age upon marriage Mistress Barnes' attitude hardens further – 'How old so ere I was, yet you shall tarry' (2.1.654–5). Mistress Barnes sees the intervention by her son Phillip over the marriage issue as further confirmation of her husband's bad faith – 'Thou set'st thy son to scoff and mock at me' (2.2.722). Order is restored only after several rancorous confrontations and some farcical crashing around the countryside in the dark. The happy ending consists of the wives being shamed into remorse by Sir Ralph Smith, a member of the local gentry and clearly a more powerful male than either of their husbands.

The dramatic presentation of the widow in Shakespeare's day worked on the basic assumption that women are foolish by nature and that this folly completely overtakes them when there is no husband to restrain it – a failing particularly evident in the older woman. Thomas Becon provided bracing advice to 'such widows as are ancient, old aged' that they should 'apply their minds unto the exercises of spiritual and heavenly things [...]' and pointed out that those who 'set their minds on fleshly pleasures', marrying and giving their money to younger husbands, ended up as deserted 'old and toothless wives'.[6] But, as I've already noted, it was the possibility of financial independence in widowhood which sparked major masculine concerns and which was reflected in literature and drama. Sir John Davies' poetic satire 'A Contention Betwixt a Wife, a Widow and a Maid' (1608) presents a debate between a widow, a young unmarried woman and a wife over which one has the most enviable lifestyle.[7] The other women point out

---

6 Thomas Becon, 'Of the Office of Widows', *Catechism*, (London: 1564) in *Understanding Hamlet: A Student Casebook to Issues, Sources, and Historical Documents*, ed. Richard Corum, (Westport, CT: Greenwood Press, 1998), 203.

7 Sir John Davies, 'A Contention Betwixt a Wife, a Widow, and a Maid For Precedence at an Offering' (1608), in *The Poems of Sir John Davies*, ed. Robert Krueger (Oxford: Clarendon Press, 1975), 216–24.

all that the widow is missing in her solitary state: she has no husband to support her; she is no longer mistress of her family; she has lost the first flush of youth; she no longer enjoys love; she can fall prey to fortune-hunting suitors; she is an object of pity. All this mirrors and reinforces the messages of the advice tracts and other contemporary literature. The unkindest cut is delivered by the wife – 'Go widow, make some younger brother rich, / And then take thought and die, and all is well' (111–12).

But the widow answers back in strong, subversive style. She admits the 'worth' (169) of her dead husband, it's true, but at a stage in the poem when we wonder if she is acknowledging his character, or reflecting on the amount he has left her. Clearly she relishes her freedom and in doing so denigrates the married state. Every wife is 'a slave' (31) but, she says, 'I have my livery sued and I am free' (32). She no longer needs the support of a husband but now 'rules alone' (46) and 'stands alone' (54), made independent by her inheritance – 'My husband's fortunes all survive to me' (150). As for love, 'the widow is awaked out of that dream' (62). Married love is imaged here as an ephemeral ideal or a fantasy, marriage itself mocked as a prison – 'Wives are as birds in golden cages kept' (77). The widow celebrates her own escape – 'Widows are birds out of these cages leapt, / Whose joyful notes make all the forest ring' (79–80).

Far from being cast down about her loss of youth the widow presents herself as being 'like a mild sweet eventide' (104). This could stand as a very proper image of a respectable dame offering restful company, but a more sensual image is superimposed by her saying that widows are also like 'good wine, which time makes better much' (162). This is explored further when the women discuss the sexual side of marriage: the widow and wife from experience. The wife, very correctly, insists that if she were widowed her 'merry days were past' (189), but the widow offers a less dismal scenario, 'Nay, then you first become sweet pleasure's guest' (190), and adds provocatively, 'Then sure it is that widows live in bliss' (206). She seems to be suggesting that pleasure does offer its invitations to those in her situation, implying opportunities for sexual satisfaction.

This is an interesting image of a woman made independent by her inheritance but Davies doesn't develop it further. The contention is resolved by the women drawing the argument to a close themselves when the wife warns them to stop rather than be seen in public as 'chattering pies' (230–31). So their discussion of the marital state has been purely private and beyond this the women police themselves so that attitudes challenging male rule are not publicly aired.

Early Modern plays which handle the public behaviour of the ageing widow tend to highlight her dangerous folly and poor judgement when she tries to run her life without essential masculine guidance. Both Middleton's *The Phoenix* (1604) and Robert Armin's *The Two Maids of Mortlake* (1608) show how the self-willed behaviour of widowed mothers causes problems for their respective sons. When choosing her second husband Castiza, in *The Phoenix*, disobediently disregards the recommendations of her friends and more importantly does not consult her son, Fidelio. The young man is concerned for her – 'that marriage knew nothing of my mind, / It never flourished in any part of my affection' (1.1.159–60) – and with just cause as Castiza's choice, the Captain, is not a good catch. After a brief experience of matrimony he is eager to go back to sea and tries to cut his losses by selling Castiza on to another suitor. Fidelio's intervention 'in the stainless quarrel of her reputation' (2.1.11) rescues this mutinous mother from the worst effects of her selfish choice. The supposedly widowed Lady, in Armin's reworking of *Hamlet*, may seem to be acting selflessly in marrying Sir William Vergir so that her son Humil can in turn marry Sir William's daughter but it is clear that she puts her own security first, making sure that her marriage settlement – 'three hundred by the year' (8.15) – is safe before pleading Humil's cause. She is also interested in her own sexual satisfaction, for although the reappearance of the husband she thought dead threatens this Lady's security she smuggles him into her household and into her bed – urging him 'Leave all to me. Women that wade in sin / Have their wits charter to authorise it' (6.34–5). Discovering the two together and not realising this is his father Humil informs Vergir and, as in *Antonio's Revenge*, the *Hamlet* plot is amusingly tweaked. Here, the stepfather urges the son to vengeance with the mother as prospective murder victim. Fortunately, Humil – like Fidelio – is a sensible son and confronts his disobedient mother so that the truth is revealed. Humil then acts with the Lady to foil Vergir's nasty schemes, and again we see the dangerous consequences of a mother's selfishness averted by the actions of a decent son.

This kind of rescue also takes place in Middleton's *The Puritan or the Widow of Watling Street* (1606) where his newly-widowed heroine rejects a respectable suitor and also falls for a worthless Captain. This mature widow's poor judgement is apparent from the start when she turns down the entirely appropriate wooer who happens to be the choice of her brother-in-law, the responsible male of the family. Here Middleton also touches on another cause for concern about widows. This woman is fearful that she won't find such an easy-going spouse next time around – 'I had keys of all, kept all, received all, had money in my purse, spent what I would [...] Oh, my sweet husband! I shall never have the like' (1.1.110–13, 114). This gives an indication as to why the widow's folly must be emphasised. Any measure of independence that has been allowed by a husband within marriage is worrying in a widow now lacking, indeed rejecting, male guidance. Having ignored good, masculine, advice and chosen her Captain this widow is publicly shamed by his arrest but her spurned suitor is on hand to save her good name by offering marriage. The folly of the widow is averted by her menfolk and she returns to the controlling structure of family life.

Jonson also highlights the seemingly perilous errors of the ageing widow, Dame Purecraft, in *Bartholomew Fair* (1614). She is daft enough to acknowledge astrological predictions that her next spouse will be a 'gentleman madman' (1.2.58), thus causing concern to her daughter and son-in-law. Yet, though he presents Dame Purecraft as a dangerously foolish older woman who has even taken the hypocritical Puritan, Zeal-of-the-land Busy, as her spiritual adviser, Jonson also reveals that she has been using this religious connection to feather her own nest. She has become 'a devourer, instead of a distributor, of the alms' (5.2.64–5). She also confesses that she has been stringing her suitors along as a good financial investment – 'I have been a wilful holy widow only to draw feasts and gifts from my entangled suitors' (5.2. 61–3).

And she is well aware of Busy's hypocrisy – 'I know him to be the capital knave of the land' (5.2.77–8). She admits all this to Quarlous, who is disguised as a lunatic and thus has won her heart. So, in spite of the concealed cunning which has enabled the Dame to achieve a substantial fortune – 'I am worth six thousand pound' (5.2.57–8) – she is still stupidly taken in by the prediction and is entirely bowled over by the phoney madman – 'I love him o' the sudden' (4.6.195). Jonson utilises several stereotypes here; that of the foolish widow, the widow determined to achieve and maintain financial security, and the sexually insatiable widow – 'and shall love him more and more' (4.6.197). The latter stereotypical characteristic results in Dame Purecraft's remarriage and although Quarlous is only feigning lunacy the implication is that the widow with wealth is a danger to herself and an inappropriate social model. Far better to be under the control of a madman, even, than operating on her own.

The dangers of disobedience in a woman, whatever her age, are often explored in the plays of Shakespeare's day but the examples I've presented here emphasise particular concerns about controlling the older woman. Despite her outspokenness an old wife on stage can still be contained by a sharp-witted spouse or some other concerned male – though in reality her dependent financial situation would doubtless be of greater relevance. However, the ageing moneyed widow is obviously a potential problem as her portrayal in plays as helpless, hopeless and lust-driven suggests. Certainly this stereotype sorts ill with what we know of the 'real lives' of Early Modern widows.

Power Mad and Passionate

Any old woman pursuing her own interests – seeking power, or sexual satisfaction, or both – is presented as entirely selfish on the Early Modern stage with family members usually the victims of her avarice and opportunism. For example, the agenda of a power-seeking woman like Catherine, the murderous Queen Mother in Marlowe's *The Massacre at Paris* (1593), is to govern no matter which son is on the throne – 'For I'll rule in France, but they shall wear the crown, / And if they storm,

I then may pull them down' (11.43–4). Shakespeare's *King John* (1596) features another power-hungry mother, Queen Eleanor. She is described by John's enemies as 'An Ate stirring him to blood and strife' (2.1.63) and this image, which links her to the instigator of moral blindness in humanity, is apt. At first she appears just high-handed, briskly identifying Philip the Bastard as her illegitimate grandson and urging him to follow her – 'I am a soldier and now bound to France' (1.1.150) – leaving John with little option but to agree and knight the newcomer. Once in France, though, Eleanor dominates the negotiations, claiming to have evidence that will refute young Arthur's claim to the English throne and pressing John into tactical agreement with the opposition – 'Urge them while their souls / Are capable of this ambition' (2.1.476–7). That she uses her son to gain power for herself is emphasised by her suspicions that Arthur's mother, Constance, is just such a manipulator – 'Thy bastard shall be king / That thou mayst be a queen and check the world' (2.1.122–3). Clearly, her behaviour has undermined her own son who remains weak and vacillating after her death. Indeed, he seems lost without her driving force – his doleful 'What, Mother dead?' (4.2.127) is repeated in line 180, 'My Mother dead!' Interestingly, another maternal figure in *King John* also demonstrates moral weakness. Lady Falconbridge furiously denies the Bastard's accusation about his real parentage, to defend her honour, only to admit the truth – 'King Richard Coeur-de-Lion was thy father' (2.1.253) – when she learns that her son is now a knight and is rejecting any claim to her husband's estate, so leaving the field clear for her legitimate offspring.

In the character of Cornelia in Webster's *The White Devil*, we see an ageing, widowed mother driven by fear of losing the little power and influence that she possesses through her family. She may seem the model of good parenting by intervening in the seduction of her married daughter, Vittoria, by Duke Bracciano, yet we are soon made aware that it's not because of outraged morality. Overhearing the lovers Cornelia initially panics – '[…] I find our house / Sinking to ruin' (1.2. 216–17) – and this fear of the destruction of 'our house' (the family, family honour and her own security) influences her outspoken attack on the Duke. Yet Webster presents this older mother as devious in her dismay.

While listening to the lovers' fond but illicit wooing, Cornelia also
overhears Vittoria's account of a supposed dream in which her husband
and Bracciano's wife are killed. It's this which presents the bad mother
with an alternative to family downfall. While apparently moralising,
Cornelia reminds the Duke of his role as exemplar of good behaviour
and highlights his power as a manipulator:

> The lives of princes should like dials move,
> Whose regular example is so strong,
> They make the times by them go right or wrong.
>
> (1.2.287–9)

It is telling that this nudge comes just after mention of the arrival of
the Duke's wife. Under the guise of appropriate maternal disapproval
Cornelia is in fact hinting at a solution. Her harping on death, funerals
and graves and the control that powerful men can have over 'right or
wrong' confirms Vittoria's supposed dream as the way for Bracciano to
solve his problem. As the Duke leaves he calls for Doctor Julio to attend
on him and Julio is the man who later arranges the poisoning of the
Duchess. Braccianio's final words to Cornelia are telling:

> Uncharitable woman, thy rash tongue
> Hath raised a fearful and prodigious storm, –
> Be thou the cause of all ensuing harm.
>
> (1.2.305–7)

This sounds like a bad conscience manufacturing an excuse – he
can focus blame for whatever he decides to do on the behaviour and
'rash tongue' of the stereotypical older woman. However, he has also
recognised and acknowledged the lack of charity and fearful fixity of
purpose in the storm-stirring Cornelia.

As a bad mother Cornelia's moral standards are influenced by self-
consideration and we see similar selfishness in Middleton's *The Revenger's
Tragedy* (1606) where another widowed mother, Gratiana, agrees to sell
her own daughter, Castiza, to the Duke's son. Gratiana's weak and

wicked behaviour also emerges from anxiety about her own security for her husband has not left her financially comfortable – 'Indeed he was a worthy gentleman/ Had his estate been fellow to his mind' (1.1.122–3). So Gratiana's son, Vindice, who is cunningly disguised, can play upon her anxieties to bring about the betrayal. His old mother is 'touched [...] nearly' (2.1.108) by his arguments but succumbs entirely at the sight of the first instalment of hard cash. She addresses the money most lovingly – '[...] these are / The means that govern our affections [...]' doting on its 'comfortable shine' and reflecting 'I blush to think what for your sakes I'll do' (2.1.123–8). Gratiana's limited moral values are exposed in a comically muddled yet revealing speech when she airily sets aside Castiza's concerns about her honour. According to Gratiana the young woman's illicit liaison with the royal offspring will raise her above the 'mean people, ignorant people' (2.1.150) who value honour and into the society of 'The better sort' who 'cannot abide it' (2.1.151). When confronted with her crime by both her sons, Vindice and Hippolito, Gratiana duly repents, weeping and praying for forgiveness. The stage directions state that the brothers are armed and that both have hold of their mother, but even without this indication of the dynamics of the scene it is clear Gratiana is physically overwhelmed and in fear for her life – 'What mean my sons? What, will you murder me?' (4.4.2). This violent image – reminiscent of Hamlet's threatening behaviour to his mother (3.4.21) – apparently redirects Gratiana on to the correct moral path.

Even in comedies a mother cannot get away with selfishness in pursuing her own interests at the expense of an offspring's concerns. Beaumont's *The Knight of the Burning Pestle* (1607) shows Mistress Merrythought repudiating her grown son Jasper, spoiling her younger son Michael and then deserting the family home. Her attitude to her husband gives an entirely inappropriate example of female behaviour to Michael:

> Let thy father go snick-up.
> He shall never come between a pair of sheets with me
> Again while he lives.
>
> (2.81–3)

Her punishment is to find the outside world less than appealing and after losing her jewels she has to return to home and husband where, ironically, the rejected Jasper pleads for and gains her re-admittance.

Though Middleton's *A Chaste Maid in Cheapside* (1611) is also a comedy it's a very dark one and here the mother, Maudlin Yellowhammer, shifts from being a source of comic embarrassment for her son to being 'a cruel mother' (4.2.59) to her daughter Moll, forcing her into a loveless marriage. Unmoved by Moll's apparent death Maudlin bustles off to fix up a soundly-financed match for son Tim – 'We'll not lose all at once, somewhat we'll catch' (5.2.116). She gets her comeuppance here for Tim marries a whore believing her to be a rich gentlewoman and when the truth is revealed the rueful Maudlin can only advise her son to make the best of a bad job – 'There's no remedy now Tim' (5.4.110). Middleton makes it clear that Maudlin's callous attitude to Moll is rooted in sexual jealousy of her daughter. She boasts, 'When I was of your youth, I was lightsome and quick two years before I was married' (1.1.8–9), but her youth has gone, of course. The destructive potential of such maternal envy is seen more dramatically in *The Turk* (1607) by John Mason. The ageing Timoclea is rejected by Mulleus as 'not pleasing' even though she reckons herself to be as attractive as ever – 'fresh and delightsome' (3.4.65). So when the Turk falls for her daughter instead Timoclea promptly murders the young woman.

Although the daughters of Queen Bonduca commit suicide with her in John Fletcher's *Bonduca* (1613) it is implied that the country suffers most as this mature, widowed ruler attempts to take on a man's role. The playwright images the invading Roman forces in positive ways, against 'certain negative values' of a Britain ruled by a woman.[8] Bonduca's folly and her failure as ruler are encapsulated in the way she has to be regularly schooled in what she says and does by an outraged male relative. This is her cousin Caratach, who tackles his task with

---

8 Paul D. Green, 'Theme and Structure in Fletcher's *Bonduca*', *Studies in English Literature* 22 (1982): 305–16 (305).

increasing frustration as he tries to right the wrongs she has done. He intervenes in the harsh treatment she, and her daughters, mete out to captives and countermands her orders. Caratach, we are given to understand, is a bluff, honest soldier attempting to run a decent, honourable war against the Romans in the face of constant female subversion and manipulation.

It is her misappropriation of male, military language that highlights Bonduca's lack of fitness as a ruler, particularly when she unsuccessfully seeks the support of her gods at the druid temple. The Queen's appeal for help is rooted in dark images – 'claps of thunder / Hang on our armed carts: and 'fore our troops / Despair and death' (3.19–21). But her entreaties are set aside as 'fretful prayers' and 'whinings' by Caratach who asserts that 'The gods love courage armed with confidence' (3.1.53, 54, 55). It is he who has the right kind of manly and robust language in which to petition – 'Give us this day good hearts, good enemies, / Good blows o'both sides' (3.1.65–6). Bonduca does not learn from this example, but demands to speak to the god again and has to be put in her place:

> **Caratach.** Tempt him no more.
> **Bonduca.** I would know further, cousin.
> **Caratach.** His hidden meaning dwells in our endeavours,
>   Our valours are our best gods.
>
> (3.1.80–83)

In trying to be manly the Queen has misjudged the language of leadership and we see her further failure when the battle goes against her and she tries to stem the tide of fleeing Britons – 'Back, cowards! / Hares, fearful hares, doves in your angers' (3.5.148–9).

Eventually Bonduca takes her own life rather than surrender to the Romans and there is strength and dignity in her death. Her rich yet measured language in addressing the Romans suggests that she and her daughters are about to be liberated and, at the same time, be empowered by death:

> In spite of all your eagles' wings, we'll work
> A pitch above you; and from our height we'll stoop
> [...]
> As if we prayed on heartless doves.
>
> (4.4.74–7)

However, Fletcher ensures that she dies at the end of Act 4 with another act to come in which her character is marginalised in favour of that of Caratach. He is now established as 'the play's true centre',[9] and acknowledged as a worthy ally by the Romans – 'through the camp, in every tongue, / The virtues of great Caratach be sung!' (5.3.203–4). Indeed, Act 5 opens with this virtuous leader rehearsing all his country's sufferings and laying these firmly at Bonduca's door:

> Oh, thou woman,
> Thou agent for adversities, what curses
> This day belong to thy improvidence!
>
> (5.1.3–5)

As I've already indicated, all ageing women seeking sexual satisfaction are presented as problematic on stage but this is particularly worrying when they are mothers who demonstrate an entirely inappropriate disregard for their own reputation and that of their offspring. The widowed Eugenia, Queen Mother of Spain, in *Lust's Dominion or The Lascivious Queen* (1600) attributed to Thomas Dekker, John Day and William Haughton, is accused by her son, Philip, of creating a 'brothelry' in the bedchamber (1.2.118) and even her plotting to regain power at court is based on the assumption that everyone else shares her own unbridled sexuality. In the end she is entirely and unbelievably reconciled with her son and expresses due repentance. Sent into solitary

---

9 Clifford Leech, *The John Fletcher Plays* (London: Chatto and Windus, 1962), 167.

confinement she agrees to 'spin out the remnant of my life, / In true contrition for my past offences' (5.3.177–8).

The dangerous nature of uncontrollable female passion is particularly emphasised in the character of the ageing widow. However, in George Chapman's *The Widow's Tears* (1605), a play not generally taken to be sympathetic to widows, I feel the playwright goes some way towards undercutting the stereotype of the lust-driven widow. When Cynthia's husband, Lysander, decides to test his wife's vow to remain chaste in widowhood by faking his own death, her initial demonstration of 'an ecstasy of sorrow' (4.1.37) would seem to fit male requirements. Alas, she fails her husband's next test when he successfully seduces her, disguised as a soldier. Cynthia has fasted for five days and is 'weak and quickly seiz'd with swooning and passions' (4.2.23) – a nudging image of a woman desperate for sex after lengthy self-denial. However, she does not immediately fling herself into the soldier's arms, as might be expected were she driven by lust, but only succumbs when she has consumed much of Lysander's handy bottle of spirits. Chapman seems uncomfortable with the idea of the mature Cynthia undone by lust alone and provides the demon drink as a substantial cause of her fall from perfection.

Once she learns how she has been tricked she rallies to protect her reputation. Bravely refusing to hide behind her 'frailties' and the hope that her 'mightiest friends' (5.1.334, 330) will defend her from Lysander, Cynthia decides to tough it out – 'I resolve to sit out one brunt more' (4.1.335). She turns on Lysander with all the fury of a wronged wife who saw through her husband's disguise right from the start but played along with him to find out just how far he would go. So Cynthia gets away with her adultery of sorts and the playwright reserves his mockery for the mortified Lysander – 'What have I done?' (5.1.488).

In a similar fashion the wealthy widow Lady Goldenfleece in Middleton's *No Wit No Help Like A Woman's* (1613) is initially presented as a woman propelled by her passions. Her experiences highlight both aspects of the widow stereotype as she is 'the object of a hunt motivated by her wealth' but also 'the wealthy (and lusty) hunter of a younger spouse'.[10] This mature woman is the comic victim of a revenge plot by the Low-Waters who have been impoverished by her late husband. Mistress Low-Water disguises herself as a young man and Lady Goldenfleece feels immediate attraction – 'The more I look on him the more I thirst for't' (2.1.207). Like Chapman, though, Middleton challenges the stereotype of the lust-driven widow for this lady understands her own feelings very well and is determined not to relinquish self-control:

> Fly from my heart all variable thoughts.
> She that's enticed by every pleasing object
> Shall find small pleasure, and as little rest.
>
> (2.1.268–70)

She also acknowledges the prior claim of her wooer Sir Gilbert and determines, with integrity, not to back out of the match – 'This knave hath lov'd me long; he's best and worthiest, / I cannot but in honour see him requited' (2.1.271–2).

But when Sir Gilbert is revealed as plotting a seduction elsewhere Lady Goldenfleece turns on him in righteous anger, not only appalled by his lusting after another behind her back but badly frightened to learn he was planning to spend her fortune on 'adulterous surfeits' (2.1.369). She is grateful to have escaped this fate and decides now to marry to satisfy her own needs and desires instead, and chooses the young man who has won her heart. Her disappointed suitors wreak an unpleasant revenge, hijacking the celebratory masque and, in disguise, denouncing the bad behaviour of all widows. Sir Gilbert, masked as Fire, expounds on the theme of the widow so driven by lust that her judgement is undermined, resulting in her choosing a second husband not 'by gravity' but through 'tricks of blood' (4.2.64, 65). The speech

---

10 Dorothea Kehler, 'Shakespeare's Widows of a Certain Age: Celibacy and Economics', in *In Another Country: Feminist Perspectives on Renaissance Drama*, ed. Dorothea Kehler and Susan Barker (Metchen, NJ: The Scarecrow Press, 1991), 23.

condemns the widow's sexuality as unpleasant, unwholesome and unnatural, thus exposing male fears about female desires. Of course, Sir Gilbert personifies the double standard – his own desires being entirely dishonest. The other suitors, disguised as the other elements, attack the widow as untrustworthy, weak and inconstant. She is even seen as tainted by the way in which her first husband made his money – more male hypocrisy, as such inherited wealth supposedly makes any widow an appealing marriage prospect. Lady Goldenfleece has to be rescued from this degrading situation by a quick-witted man, Beveril, and she is powerless to take issue with the accusations made. Her only recourse is to pass the whole thing off as a joke (4.3.167–70) but this is a sour scene.

The articulation of so many male fears about wealthy widows shows the vulnerability of a woman suddenly confronted, in a masque, with unmasked male aggression. Lady Goldenfleece suffers further such aggression but this time from a female, the disguised Mistress Low-Water who becomes her second 'husband'. There is much wedding-night comedy as the sexually aroused widow pursues her new spouse only to be rejected – 'A married man must think of other matters' (5.1.9) – but, like the wit of the masque, these comic moments also carry discomfort. The widow grovels and begs for her husband's favour, reflecting sadly, 'I chose you for love, / Youth, and content of heart, and not for troubles' (5.1.37–8). In dramatizing this passionate widow's plight Middleton demonstrates the insidious nature of male fears about the ageing, lone female whilst also reinforcing received wisdom that wealthy widows are always at risk and that best safety lies in sensible remarriage. Luckily for Lady Goldenfleece a saviour and eventual spouse is on hand in the person of the stalwart Beveril, so the conclusion of this play also seems to confirm the received wisdom of the age – that the only good widow was a married one.

Part III

SHAKESPEARE'S SUBVERSION OF THE STEREOTYPES

'Wayward' Wives

As I've shown, Shakespeare certainly wasn't above accessing the old wife stereotype in his plays. But in two of them, *The Merry Wives of Windsor* and *All Is True (Henry VIII)*, which he wrote with Fletcher, there is a definite movement beyond the stereotype. In each play we find sympathetic engagement with what happens to a woman when she faces a crisis in her marriage – a crisis made more acute because she is ageing. This powerfully imaginative approach argues a sensitive dramatic response to female old age.

Though these two plays are very different in many respects, both present mature wives handling situations which threaten their emotional lives, their social status and their autonomy within marriage. Mistress Page and Mistress Ford triumph over the threat embodied in the fat stalker Falstaff by apparently being wicked wives while in fact setting their own, very moral behavioural agenda. In contrast, Queen Katherine loses her status despite being all that a good wife should be, and to add to her tragedy the attack upon her is initiated by the very person who is supposed to care for and support her. She becomes disobedient and – albeit briefly – outspokenly disloyal and she maintains until her death the political and personal position she has chosen.

Although it's a comedy, like the best of the genre *The Merry Wives of Windsor* skates close to disaster for some of the characters. The engaging story cannot conceal the fact that these mature wives, Margaret Page and Alice Ford, face public shame if their plans go wrong. Falstaff, an intruder into the domestic sphere, is no sly and secretive sinner and his scheme to entrap the wives is well aired with various fellow conmen and other interested parties. The whole purpose of such trophy hunting is to advertise the continuing sexual potency of the male concerned so the reputations of these mature wives are very much at risk. Exploration of the community policing of morality in Elizabethan times reveals the way in which libellous publications and slanderous gossip could stir up local communities – particularly when the focus was on accusations about wives cuckolding their husbands. In such cases injured parties would often go to law, demonstrating the very real threat posed to married women.[1] It is also telling that *The Merry Wives of Windsor* is set within a rural community for York Church Court records suggest that more of 'the rural middling sort' were involved in defamation cases brought on sexual matters.[2] It seems that the Early Modern English villager would be well aware 'that reputations are more easily lost than gained'.[3] Certainly both merry wives have to take considerable care when they 'wage an undercover women's war' in this play.[4]

Yet it's clear that whatever scandal might fly around about Meg Page, her husband George would not believe it. Their relationship is Shakespeare's only representation on stage of a comfortable marriage and it's interesting that he chooses a mature couple to embody this enviable state. That the Pages use first names in public is an indication of mutual friendship. They may hold contrary views on a suitable husband for their daughter and scheme to outwit each other over this but there is no malice involved and no bad feeling between them when they find their plans overturned. Fenton is accepted as their

---

1 See F. G. Emmison, *Elizabethan Life: Disorder* (Chelmsford: Essex County Council, 1970).

2 A. J. A. Sharpe, 'Defamation and Sexual Slander in Early Modern England: The Church Courts at York', *Borthwick Papers* 58 (York: Borthwick Institute of Historical Research, 1980): 15–27.

3 Ibid., 18.

4 Pamela Allen Brown, *Better a Shrew Than a Sheep: Women, Drama and the Culture of Jest in Early Modern England* (Ithaca and London: Cornell University Press, 2003), 43.

son-in-law with a combined, dignified front: after all, Anne Page has been provided with a convincing model of an equable marriage by her own parents.

Yet, Meg Page knows the importance of maintaining her good name in public and she is deeply affronted by Falstaff's assumption that she has been leading him on:

> What an unweigh'd behaviour hath this Flemish drunkard
> picked – with the devil's name – out of my conversation, that
> he dares in this manner assay me?
>
> (2.1.21–4)

But despite her denunciation of such unpleasant male activity – 'Why, I'll exhibit a bill in Parliament for the putting down of men' (2.1.27–8) – she still tends to blame some 'unweigh'd behaviour' of her own for Falstaff's outrageous actions. Mistress Page assumes Falstaff 'is able to see something in her, that she herself is unable to see [...]', an '[...] unclean thing [...]'.[5] Even a strong-minded, mature wife, secure in her husband's trust, finds it difficult to break away from the judgement of her society that 'Frailty, thy name is woman' (*Hamlet*, 1.2.146).

Mistress Ford is much less fortunate in her marriage and sadly aware that her friend is 'the happier woman' (2.1.101). Ford's jealousy has nothing to do with passionate attachment to Alice – he focuses on 'avoiding being known as a cuckold, not clearing his wife'.[6] Thinking to trap her with Falstaff he disguises himself as a rival lecherous wooer and his language here shows that his notion of love is based on getting value for money. He announces he has 'bought many presents', 'given largely', 'purchased at an infinite rate' (2.2.193, 194, 199–200). He is also pathologically pessimistic about human nature in general and women's behaviour in particular and is easily convinced that his wife and Mistress Page are unfaithful. He takes

---

5 Natasha Korda, *Shakespeare's Domestic Economies Gender and Property in Early Modern England* (Philadelphia: University of Pennsylvania Press, 2002), 88.

6 Brown, 53.

a morbid pleasure in anticipating the public revelation of this when he can 'torture' his wife and 'pluck the borrowed veil of modesty from the so-seeming Mistress Page' (3.2.35–6). Ford's venting of his frustration on the Old Woman of Brentford by administering a thrashing (4.2) is funny because we know this is Falstaff being smuggled out of the Ford house in disguise, but it is also disturbing in terms of the furious husband's violent rage. The Ford marriage is clearly uncomfortable and unstable and it is easy to imagine a man so lacking in self-control devising many forms of 'torture' (3.2.35) for a wife who displeases him.

It's not only the reputation of each woman which is at risk through Falstaff's lecherous meddling. Shakespeare makes it clear that both wives have a measure of financial independence within marriage. Falstaff quickly ascertains that Mistress Ford 'has all the rule of her husband's purse' and Mistress Page 'bears the purse too' (1.3.47–8, 61). This would clearly add considerably to the pleasures of seduction for this impecunious knight, but any tarnishing of a good name would probably result in the loss of this autonomy for the wives so Falstaff, though an obvious scoundrel, is a very real threat to their hard-won, yet easily damaged, reputations. They could, of course, hand over to others the options for retributive action – in such situations 'kin and neighbors could serve as a woman's primary defense [...]'.[7] Instead they decide to play the bold but dangerous game of pretending to be stereotypically disobedient, disloyal wives. The results of course make for splendid comic moments on stage as Falstaff is beaten up, squashed into a basket of dirty washing, dumped in the river and later tormented by 'fairies' in the forest, while Mistress Page and Mistress Ford publicly demonstrate that 'Wives may be merry and yet honest too' (4.2.94).

Although the Ford relationship is seriously flawed, at the end of the play we are shown this mature married couple continuing to struggle along together as Ford announces his intention to 'lie with Mistress Ford' that night and presumably on future nights too (5.5.237).

---

7   Brown, 52.

In *Henry VIII* though, we have an exploration of the difficult territory of the separation and divorce of a mature married couple – a couple who are also King and Queen of England.

Katherine is a complex character who engages our interest and sympathy thanks to the playwrights' subtle assessment of her position, first as valued mature wife and then as rejected marriage partner. They show her keen awareness that, just like her less elevated contemporaries, she owes her position in the world to that of her husband. If he divorces her on his terms she loses that position, her own good name and the legitimacy of her only surviving child. Her royal background, her 'friends in Spain' (2.4.53), even the regular public affirmations of her good character, from the Second Gentleman (2.1.158) to the King himself (2.4.133–40), will count for little if she forfeits her place as Henry's wife. She will, indeed, be turned 'into nothing' (3.1.113). In emphasising the length of her relationship with Henry the dramatists make an issue of Katherine's age to present a moving and powerful account of an old wife's response to the sudden withdrawal of marital security.

Her first appearance in Act 1 establishes the strength of Katherine's position as Henry's wife and the Queen of England. She is clearly obedient and loyal and speaks out only in the furtherance of her husband's good. Henry's gracious 'Half your suit / Never name to us: you have half our power' (2.1.11–12) could simply be public politeness but his acceptance of her subsequent advice shows that he relies on Katherine in political situations. She loyally points out Wolsey's introduction of new taxation for which Henry will be blamed publicly and when the Cardinal argues, it's the Queen who challenges him. She takes a hard line with Wolsey, using strong, emphatic language to describe the responses to his actions – 'not wholesome', 'pestilent', 'tongues spit', 'curses now live', 'incensed will' (1.2.46, 50, 61, 63–4, 66) – while Henry can be detached, puzzled yet concerned – 'Taxation? / [...] what taxation?' (1.2.38–9). So when Wolsey attempts to defend his position, Henry, independent of the sharp rebukes of his wife to his minister, is able to weigh in with sound, measured advice for the Cardinal (1.2.89–103) which is immediately acted upon.

Katherine's personal dislike of Wolsey is evident but in challenging him she also demonstrates 'empathy for the plight of her downtrodden subjects'.[8] However, it's important to be aware that her outspokenness here is clearly allowed by Henry. She is permitted to play the role of the good wife who is a little too voluble but only out of love for her husband and care for the good balance of his rule – a situation which emphasises the bond of trust between them.

She is less active when the Duke of Buckingham's alleged treachery is investigated. Her only interventions are important though. Once again she rebukes the over-eager Wolsey – this time for his lack of 'charity' (1.2.143) – and in her questioning of the surveyor she alerts Henry to the fact that the man's evidence may be suspect:

> You were the Duke's surveyor, and lost your office
> On the complaint o'th'tenants. Take good heed
> You charge not in your spleen a noble person
> And spoil your nobler soul – I say take heed;
>
> (1.2.173–6)

The surveyor sensibly picks up the cue and duly swears to tell the truth, putting his evidence on a proper footing. Having a wife as sharp-witted and loyal as Katherine to watch his back is an advantage to the King and she clearly has his confidence.

However, Katherine's loyalty gives way to unexpected defiance when Henry, now pursuing Anne Boleyn, initiates divorce proceedings in Act 2. The Queen's appearance before the court presents a powerful visual image in itself. The proceedings open in lavish style with trumpets heralding a grand stage procession of vergers; scribes; the Archbishop of Canterbury; the Bishops of Lincoln, Ely, Rochester and St Asaph; a gentleman bearing the great seal and a cardinal's hat; two priests

---

8 Alison Thane, "'O, lawful let it be / That I have room... to curse awhile'": Voicing the Nation's Conscience in Female Complaint in *Richard III*, *King John* and *Henry VIII*', in *This England, That Shakespeare: New Angles on Englishness and the Bard*, ed. Willy Maley and Margaret Tudeau-Clayton (Farnham: Ashgate, 2010), 105–26 (123).

each carrying a silver cross; a gentleman usher with a sergeant-at-arms carrying a silver mace; two gentlemen carrying two great silver pillars; then Cardinals Wolsey and Campeius (the Pope's representative); and two noblemen with the sword and the mace. Henry follows on, taking his seat under the cloth of state and the two Cardinals sit a little below him as judges (2.4). All the 'big guns' are rolled out with all the male power on display so it is telling, and particularly dramatic, that Katherine appears attended only by one gentleman usher. She's supposed to be there to rubber-stamp the King's wishes of course, but she ignores the court proceedings and kneeling directly before her husband begs for an adjournment. In doing so she publicises her own record as a good wife in language which is restrained, careful and well-argued. She presents her case as a partner of 'Upward of twenty years' to Henry (2.4.34), and at first her tone is personal – 'Alas, sir, / In what have I offended you?' (2.4.16–17) and she goes on:

> Heaven witness
> I have been to you a true and humble wife,
> At all times to your will conformable,
> Ever in fear to kindle your dislike
>
> (2.4. 20–23)

This image of an obedient wife is enhanced by her mention of the 'many children' she bore Henry (2.4.35) and the very fact that she does not discuss the fate of these offspring is suggestive of private loss and grief shared between husband and wife. Moving from these intimate memories she challenges Henry to prove 'against mine honour aught' (2.3.37) and then shifts her discourse from the personal to the political, engaging with the arrangement of their marriage by their fathers after serious thought and reference to 'wise council' (2.4.49). Katherine carefully establishes her credentials as Henry's wife and the lawful, well-grounded, nature of their marriage. She also reminds the court of her own, elevated, family background, 'My father, King of Spain, was reckoned one / The wisest prince that there had reigned [...]' (2.4.46–7).

When Wolsey enters the debate, however, Katherine's self-control wavers. At first she challenges his role as judge in the hearing, blaming him for having caused the dispute between her and her husband (2.4.76–7). Then anger and despair prevail and she lashes out at his 'arrogancy, spleen and pride' (2.4.108). When she curtsies to Henry and turns to go before the proceedings have properly begun the whole legal charade starts to totter. Cardinal Campeius describes Katherine as 'obstinate / Stubborn to justice' (2.4.119–20) then panics, hissing "Tis not well. / She's going away' (2.4.121–2). Henry orders that Katherine be called again and her usher, Griffiths, tries to persuade her to turn and face her judges – 'Madam, you are called back' (2.4.124). Her response is crushing:

> What need you note it? Pray you keep your way.
> When *you* are called, return. Now the Lord help.
> They vex me past my patience. Pray you pass on.
> I will not tarry; no nor ever more
> Upon this business my appearance make
> In any of their courts.
>
> (2.4.125–30)

She has publicly refused to obey her husband, to obey her King. Henry tries to cover this inconvenient truth, calling after her to 'Go thy ways, Kate' (2.4.130) after she has already gone, and praising her 'rare qualities, sweet gentleness, / [...] meekness saint-like, wife-like government [...] The queen of earthly queens' (2.4.135, 138). It's a thoroughly awkward eulogy to a wife who has shifted abruptly from bowing to his 'pleasure' (2.4.55) to being argumentative, vexed, impatient and finally, disobedient.

We do not see husband and wife together again but Katherine's vigour in defending her marriage and her honour is still evident in her later confrontation with Wolsey and Campeius, who try to change her mind about the divorce. She refuses to see them in private or allow any discussion in Latin, emphasising her own clear conscience and readiness to be questioned, and also underlining the fact that she has been England's Queen for some time – 'I am not such a truant since my coming / As not to know the language I have lived in' (3.1.42–3). Similarly she uses her lack of powerful friends at Court to play up her position as 'a woman, friendless, hopeless!' (3.1.79). Her careful politicking is overcome, though, by righteous anger when the two churchmen urge her to knuckle under – 'Ye turn me into nothing. Woe upon ye, / And all such false professors!' (3.1.113–14).

Ultimately Katherine's anger flares into direct and devastating criticism of her husband and his withdrawal of marital affection. All her hurt and sense of betrayal are articulated here:

> Have I with all my full affections
> Still met the King, loved him next heaven, obeyed him,
> [...]
> Almost forgot my prayers to content him,
> And am I thus rewarded?
>
> (3.1.128–32)

In her mind there is no separation between King and husband, Queen and wife and she refuses to sacrifice her marriage to political expedience:

> I dare not make myself so guilty
> To give up willingly that noble title
> Your master wed me to. Nothing but death
> Shall e'er divorce my dignities.
>
> (3.1.138–41)

This is a wife being outrageous, making a scene – she even drags in the friendless state of her women (3.1.147–9) – and embarrassing her husband through his messengers. Yet she cannot sustain this position. The only way she can touch Henry now is by doing what he wants, once more playing the role of good supportive wife as seen in Act 1. She has no other means of re-engaging his affections for, 'I am old my lords' (3.1.119).

Katherine is stripped of her titles and banished from the court so it's not surprising that when she hears of Wolsey's death she delivers a sharply-worded summary of her enemy's faults – 'Simony was fair play. / His own opinion was his law' (4.2.36–7). But she is also fair-minded enough to pray, 'So may he rest, his faults lie gently on him' (4.2.31) and to conclude, 'Peace be with him' (4.2.75). It's after forgiving her old enemy that she experiences a vision. She falls asleep but she and the audience, see six 'personages' all in white, their faces covered with golden visors, carrying bay garlands with which they do homage to Katherine. This scene is sometimes cut from modern productions of the play but it's symbolic of Katherine gaining spiritual peace shortly before her death, with the promise of heavenly favour. It also lifts her female power into the religious realm – the playwrights are preparing us for the final scene of the play.

Experiencing this promise of 'eternal happiness' (4.2.90) doesn't turn Katherine into a sunny little saint however. When a messenger arrives he addresses her as 'Your grace' and Katherine snaps 'You are a saucy fellow –/ Deserve we no more reverence?' (4.2.101–2) and pretty soon the messenger is grovelling at her feet and begging her pardon. Katherine is still Queen of England. The messenger announces an ambassador from Katherine's nephew Carlos, bringing her messages of comfort. As she tartly remarks 'Oh, my good lord, that comfort comes too late, / 'Tis like a pardon after execution' (4.2.121–2). But she realises the ambassador will be going back to King Henry's court and takes the opportunity to give him a letter she has written to her husband. Here the playwrights use Katherine's actual words as a basis for a tender farewell from this loving and forgiving wife – though adding a little touch of wit of the kind a married couple might share:

> Remember me
> In all humility unto his highness.
> Say his long trouble now is passing
> Out of this world. Tell him in death I blessed him,
> For so I will.
>
> (4.2.161–4)

Katherine's final speech is to her women urging that when she is dead they 'Strew me over/ With maiden flowers, that they may know / I was a chaste wife to my grave' (4.2.169–71).

This strong-minded old wife continues to influence the play after her death and Shakespeare and Fletcher achieve this by tweaking history. Her death in the final scene of Act 4 is followed in Act 5 scene 1 by the birth of the Princess Elizabeth who will later rule the country. In fact Katherine was still alive when Elizabeth was born but it was important for the playwrights to emphasise Katherine's legacy to Elizabeth by having the death of one strong Queen followed immediately by the birth of another. The play concludes with the onstage christening of this infant and Archbishop Cranmer revealing that Elizabeth will be a virgin Queen, 'A most unspotted lily' (5.4.60). Katherine has already described herself in the same way – 'Like the lily, / That once was mistress of the field and flourished' (3.1.150–51). The continuing image of purity in the female monarch resonates here.

The playwrights' concluding emphasis suggests a legacy from Katherine to Elizabeth but along with this symbolism it is as a disobedient and outspoken woman that Katherine impacts upon this play – an old wife struggling to hold on to herself in the face of the 'nothing' of divorce. She does this with wit and words – seemingly the only, limited, weapons of a wife stripped of the power given to her by her husband.

Much-Maligned Mothers

In the characters of Gertrude in *Hamlet* and Volumnia in *Coriolanus* we appear to have two contrasting images of motherhood: the first the personification of female 'frailty' (1.2.146), the second tougher than any of the men around her. Yet if we bear in mind that these are ageing women we can detect many similarities between them as they struggle with the problematic relationship between a mature mother and adult son. I believe Shakespeare considers this with remarkable sensitivity.

As old Hamlet's widow, wife to the new King, her former brother-in-law Claudius, and mother to young Hamlet, Gertrude is often critically imaged as the powerful and irrepressible sexual focus of the play and her position as an ageing mother becomes side-lined in reading, analysis and particularly in production. I argue that Shakespeare's Gertrude has her identity imposed upon her by the men around her and that she adapts her behaviour to suit the expectations and requirements of those she is with. I see her as a repressed female rather than an irrepressible sexpot, but the latter is more often than not the preferred image presented and embellished by male stage and film directors. While Freudian frissons fill some dramatizations of the famous 'closet scene' in Act 3 when Gertrude confronts Hamlet, Shakespeare in fact generates a sense of discomfort and danger here, not through sexual nudging but by showing a mature mother physically threatened and punished by her adult son. Though, as I've noted, there are obvious dramatic connections between Hamlet's schooling of his mother and that of Vindice and Hippolito towards Gratiana in *The Revenger's Tragedy*, Shakespeare elevates the character of Gertrude way beyond that of the stereotypical bad mother.

Focusing on the dialogue given to Gertrude we find that she 'speaks plainly, directly and chastely' and that her actions 'are as solicitous and unlascivious as her language'.[9] We should not ignore Gertrude's 'own words and deeds' in favour of what others say about her.[10] Equally her remarriage is not something anyone other than her son could damn her for – her 'activities in the months following her husband's death are unexceptional for a woman in her society [...]'.[11] However, if we do look closely at Gertrude's language and behaviour we see a woman who has so internalised male demands that, in age, the result is almost complete eradication of the self. She responds to her men on cue and at times even tries to anticipate their requirements.

There are two powerful, male-constructed stereotypes of good and bad female behaviour against which Gertrude is matched and assessed

---

9 Rebecca Smith, 'A Heart Cleft in Twain: The Dilemma of Shakespeare's Gertrude' in *The Woman's Part: Feminist Criticism of Shakespeare*, ed. Gayle Green and Carol Neely (Urbana: University of Illinois Press, 1980), 194–210 (199).

10 Ibid., 207.

11 Richard Corum, *Understanding Hamlet: A Student Casebook to Issues, Sources, and Historical Documents* (Westport, CT: Greenwood Press, 1998), 187.

by her son – firstly Hecuba, featured in the First Player's 'passionate speech' (2.2.435) and secondly the Player Queen who co-stars in *The Mousetrap*, the play Hamlet commissions with the aim of forcing a confession from Claudius (3.2). The aged Hecuba shows proper wifely devotion, running barefoot and bereft of finery to bewail the 'mincing' of her husband (2.2.508–21). The Player Queen embodies another stereotype, the woman who promises not to remarry if her husband dies before her – 'A second time I kill my husband dead / When second husband kisses me in bed' (3.2.175–6) – but is revealed as a faithless hypocrite. In Hamlet's view Gertrude is at first a Hecuba-wife to Hamlet senior:

> Why she would hang on him
> As if increase of appetite had grown
> By what it fed on,
>
> (1.2.143–5)

only to be judged even worse than 'a beast that wants discourse of reason' (1.2.150) when she remarries. The only other impression of Gertrude's behaviour as old Hamlet's wife comes from the Ghost, but while this witness describes her as 'seeming-virtuous' (1.5.46) he has more to say about her poor choice of a second husband – 'O Hamlet, what a falling off was there, / From me [...] to decline / Upon a wretch whose natural gifts were poor to those of mine' (1.5.47–8; 50–52). Interestingly, the Ghost blames her defection on Claudius and the 'witchcraft of his wit' (1.5.43) and urges his son not to take vengeance on Gertrude – 'Leave her to heaven' (1.5.86). From this we can see that Hamlet has reconstructed his mother to suit himself in his grief, while the Ghost has his own construct of this woman. Nowhere in the play does Gertrude say anything about her relationship with her first husband or the reasons for her marrying the second, and she is judged unheard – 'O most pernicious woman!' (1.5.105). I support the view that this unexamined judgement has affected the presentation of the role in countless performances of *Hamlet*.

It is important, therefore, to consider what Shakespeare reveals about Gertrude through the character herself. We are first aware of her in Act 1 scene 2 as a silent presence whose new husband is introducing her to the court. She takes no part in Claudius' justification of their marriage which is problematic because of their relationship, though not in terms of supposed speed.[12] Nor does Gertrude participate in the arrangements to deal with the threat from Fortinbras, even though her husband refers to her as 'Th'imperial jointress to this warlike state' (1.2.9) – his co-ruler. She is rather the prop to the new monarch's position: law and war remain firmly in the male domain. When Gertrude does speak at last it is in her maternal role, remonstrating with her son over his continuing public display of mourning (1.2.68–73). However, her intervention here is in support of her husband. Claudius has already announced his good intentions towards Hamlet (1.2.64) and is struggling with the uneasy role of stepfather:

> **King.**   How is it that the clouds still hang on you?
> **Hamlet.**   Not so, my lord, I am too much i' th' sun.
>
>   (1.2.66–7)

It is in backing Claudius that Gertrude picks up her husband's 'clouds' image and cuts across her son's ironic reference to 'the sun' to urge him, 'cast thy nightly colour off' (1.2.68). Her seemingly philosophical attitude to death, 'Thou know'st 'tis common – all that lives must die' (1.2.72), is hardly designed to comfort a grieving son, if her aim is to reconcile him to his father's death and her remarriage. As a wife, though, and an ageing one at that, it is important to be seen to support her new husband and her words demonstrate this. As Claudius continues the 'death-is-common' theme when he tackles Hamlet – 'But you must know your father lost a father / That father lost, lost his' (1.2.89–90) – husband and wife are shown as working as a team, indeed, as 'one flesh' (4.3.53–4). When Claudius urges Hamlet to remain at court Gertrude follows her husband's lead – 'Let not thy mother lose her prayers, Hamlet. / I pray thee stay with us, go not to Wittenburg' (1.2.118–19).

---

12 '[…] in France and England the use of mourning has ever been thirty days
   […]' Sir William Segar (1602) in Corum, 195.

This image of Gertrude as a dutiful wife continues when Claudius sets Rosencrantz and Guildenstern to spy on Hamlet. If she has concerns about this somewhat sneaky procedure she doesn't say, but echoes and reinforces her husband's request. Wifely compliance is also seen in her response to Polonius' theory of Hamlet's madness. Before the young man's love letter to Ophelia is read out Gertrude backs the favourite cause of her son's 'distemper' (2.2.55) – 'I doubt it is no other but the main, / His father's death' (2.2. 56–7). In this she is echoing Claudius' view – 'what should it be, / More than his father's death' (2.2.7–8). However, Gertrude adds to this a reason that Claudius did not touch on – 'and our o'er-hasty marriage' (2.2.57). For the first time we see Gertrude advance her own opinion – whatever the socially acceptable view of when a widow can remarry this particular relict is less than comfortable with her own 'o'er-hasty' matrimonial moves. Yet, when the men start getting excited over the notion of Hamlet as spurned lover and decide to investigate further Gertrude quickly revises her stated opinion and agrees with them. 'It may be; very likely' (2.2.153). The King's attitude now enables Gertrude to display a concern for Hamlet not permissible earlier when he was behaving badly towards his stepfather. The men have designated Hamlet as mad through unrequited love, so Gertrude can make the closest she comes to a sympathetic remark about her son – 'But look where sadly the poor wretch comes reading' (2.2.170) – without jeopardising her own position.

When Claudius and Polonius set up Ophelia as a kind of Judas-goat to trap Hamlet into revealing his feelings, Gertrude's response to her husband who has just ordered her off – 'I shall obey you' (3.1.39) – gives a clear example of correct behaviour to the young woman. Her measured words to Ophelia support what their menfolk see as an ideal solution to an awkward problem:

> And for your part, Ophelia, I do wish
> That your good beauties be the happy cause
> Of Hamlet's wildness; so shall I hope your virtues
> Will bring him to his wonted way again,
>
> (3.1.40–43)

She is well aware of her social responsibility to provide a model of obedience and order to a younger woman.

This sensitive exploration of the older woman negotiating her way through relationships with men is crucial to our understanding of the violent confrontation between Hamlet and Gertrude. She responds to her son's bullying as she has responded to men throughout the play (especially to her new husband): following, agreeing and placating. Hamlet is threatening and abusive and Gertrude frightened and confused. 'O Hamlet, thou hast cleft my heart in twain!' (3.4.147) is not, I believe, the repentant cry of a miserable mother whose beloved son has revealed her sins to her and made her sorry, but the desperation of a woman who is now deeply afraid of her son and confused by the collapse of an established pattern of behaviour in which she has always known what she must do to secure male approval.

Like Ophelia, Gertrude is set up by her menfolk for this confrontation, with Polonius and Claudius deciding on the agenda and Polonius on hand with instructions for Gertrude – 'A will come straight. Look you lay home to him' (3.4.1). As we know, the crucial interview takes place in Gertrude's closet and for some modern directors of film and theatre 'the closet is synonymous with Gertrude's bedroom'[13] with those repetitive Freudian results. However, the subject of the interview 'is hardly the stuff to be discussing while seated on the edge of your mother's bed' and some scholars consider a closet as being a personal space within a house 'where social rather than sexual intercourse takes place'.[14] So, 'the Freudian, Oedipal reading of the play emerges partially as the result of historical inattention [...]'.[15]

If we can set aside this Oedipal reading it's clear that violence is simmering in this scene. When Hamlet appears he is still wound up tight after the players' performance, where he was convinced of Claudius' guilt by the man's reactions, and his subsequent inability to act on that conviction when the King was at prayer and at his mercy. Gertrude doesn't know this, however, so her opening gambit, 'Hamlet, thou hast

---

13 Jerry Brotton, 'Ways of Seeing *Hamlet*' in *Hamlet New Critical Essays*, ed. Arthur F. Kinney, (London: Routledge 2002) 161–76, 164.

14 Ibid., 165.

15 Ibid., 165–6.

thy father much offended' (3.4.9) is unfortunate. Her son is only too aware of how he has let his father down. She attempts to re-establish an appropriate relationship between them but his answer – 'would you were not so – you are my mother' (3.4. 16) – indicates that the interview is already well off course. Faced with such a response, Gertrude is eager now to hand over the situation to someone else, retreating into the safety of female silence – 'Nay, then, I'll set those to you that can speak' (3.4.17) – but she is prevented by her son. His behaviour is alarming enough to make her fear for her life and although Shakespeare gives no stage direction as to Hamlet's actions the exchange suggests that he is detaining his mother physically:

Hamlet.   Come, come and sit you down. You shall not budge.
                                 You go not till I set you up a glass
                                 Where you may see the inmost part of you.
Queen Gertrude. What wilt thou do? Thou wilt not murder me?
                                          (3.4.18–21)

In fact it's the eavesdropping Polonius who is murdered but Shakespeare creates a frightening scene here with an ageing woman defenceless in the presence of an armed killer. That the killer is her son only exacerbates the terror. Gertrude shows considerable courage at first, attempting to stand up to Hamlet – 'What have I done, that thou dar'st wag thy tongue / In noise so rude against me?' (3.4.38–9) – and in trying to make sense of his ravings. This bravery is short-lived, though, and she is silenced by her son's aggression and made to suffer an outpouring of verbal abuse, insults and accusations, laced with images of decadent sexuality (3.4. 62–84). In desperation Gertrude, used to following the male lead, picks up on what he seems to want of her and in order to conciliate and appease she presents herself, without argument, as guilty and penitent:

                Thou turn'st my eyes into my very soul,
                And there I see such black and grained spots
                As will not leave their tinct.
                         (3.4.79–81)

Hamlet does not respond, being too tied up in his own vision of his mother's supposed lasciviousness and decadence (3.4.82–4) and Gertrude again emphasises her willingness to accept suffering if that is what he wants – 'These words like daggers enter in mine ears' (3.4.85). What she most wants, however, is for him to cease his verbal assault and be quiet, 'O Hamlet speak no more', 'O speak to me no more', 'No more, sweet Hamlet', 'No more' (3.4.78, 84, 86, 91).

Even after the intervention of his father's ghost Hamlet rants on, warning his mother to keep out of Claudius' bed and giving her a lecture on the habits of abstinence. He also remarks in passing that he regrets the murder of Polonius and he presents himself as an instrument of heaven. His reference to possible physical danger for his mother – 'break your own neck down' (3.4.180) – completes the division between them. Gertrude is very careful about her words to Hamlet here, linking and repeating 'breath' and 'life' so that her dangerous son will understand that she is far too frightened and oppressed by him to betray him:

> Be thou assured, if words be made of breath
> And breath of life, I have no life to breathe
> What thou hast said to me.
>
> (3.4.181–3)

Gertrude is not reconstituted into a good old mother through her violent schooling at Hamlet's hands. There is no suggestion that she follows her son's instructions to reject Claudius: indeed, when Laertes returns she defends her husband against him to the extent of physically trying to restrain the young man (4.5. 115–25). Gertrude may appear disobedient during the final duel scene in drinking to Hamlet's health when Claudius has forbidden her, but this is a mild defiance apparently permitted by her husband's newly supportive attitude towards her son (5.2.239). In behaving as a wife should, Gertrude seems to have weathered the upheaval caused when men change the rules of female behaviour and it is interesting to note that Hamlet also seems to accept this, paying no further attention to his mother other than cool respect. In this remarkable play we not only see the agonising of a young man attempting to become an avenger against his better nature and to gain the approval of his dead father; we also see the dangers facing an ageing woman who is entirely reliant upon the approval of men.

The desire of Volumnia in Shakespeare's *Coriolanus* to have her personal ambitions for her son fulfilled is an accepted aspect of the play which 'furnishes the stage with one of the few images of empowered old age in a woman'.[16] But the approach of her old age adds urgency and pressure and, I argue, this undermines her attempted manipulation of her son. Her motherly feelings for Coriolanus are openly passionate and possessive – 'If my son were my husband, I should freelier rejoice in that absence wherein he won honour than in the embracements of his bed where he would show most love' (1.3.2–5). Such robust sexual imagery can be seen as inappropriate, especially as she is using it to compare her own attitude to Coriolanus' absence to that of his actual wife, Virgilia. Yet it shows that Volumnia still understands herself as being powerfully connected to her son and entitled to share the honours he is winning. And although the picture conjured is of herself as subservient female recipient of her son's male 'embracements' she is soon revealed as a woman who, like Gertrude to some extent, has so thoroughly internalised traditional masculine values as to take them as a model for herself. Instead of occupying a female place within this male-dictated structure Volumnia, unlike Gertrude, has adopted and adapted male behaviour and so the mother who represents herself as her son's 'wife' is, in truth, more of a strong father figure to him.

The news of Coriolanus' triumphant return is made more splendid for Volumnia by the fact that he is wounded – 'I thank the gods for't' (2.1.119) – and she recalls the other injuries her son has amassed: she knows his victories by the body map of his scars. This masculine toughness contrasts with the care and compassion for Coriolanus expressed by older male characters in the play – Lartius urging him to rest (1.6.15–16) and Cominius later advising 'a gentle bath / And balms applied' (1.7.63–4).

---

16 Nina Taunton, 'Time's Whirligig: Images of Old Age in Coriolanus, Francis Bacon and Thomas Newton' in *Growing Old in Early Modern Europe Cultural Representations*, ed. Erin Campbell (Aldershot: Ashgate, 2006), 21–38 (22).

The masculine aspect of Volumnia's character is often identified as a crucial element of her power, along with the way she exercises control over her son.[17] She is seen as a 'cannibalistic mother who denies food yet feeds on the victories of her sweet son'[18] and as one who has 'fashioned' her son and who 'may consequently dismantle her creation'.[19] However, her age is not considered as an essential motivating influence on her behaviour even though it is something she herself draws attention to and which shifts the balance in her relationship with her son. When he returns victorious she declares:

> I have lived
> To see inherited my very wishes
> And the buildings of my fancy
> (2.1.195–7)

The linking of 'have lived' and 'inherited' looks towards her own death and she triumphantly presents herself as an ageing matriarch who has seen achieved almost everything she mapped out for her son. He just needs to attain the 'one thing wanting' in her plans, a consulship (2.1.198). Volumnia wants her son settled in an appropriate civic role which will crown his military achievements. However, this requires Coriolanus to move into a political mode of being and he warns her that he's not capable of doing this – 'I had rather be their servant in my way / Than sway with them in theirs' (2.1.199–200). She tries to coach her son but in instructing him in political dealings she shifts from her straightforward, masculine attitude into stereotypical feminine behaviour, demonstrating compliance, compromise and humility.

At first Coriolanus is coerced into being 'humble as the ripest mulberry' (3.2.79) but he can't sustain this for long. Volumnia punishes

---

17 See, for instance, Coppelia Kahn, *Roman Shakespeare: Warriors, Wounds and Women* (London: Routledge, 1997).

18 Janet Adelman, *Suffocating Mothers: Fantasies of Maternal Origin in Shakespeare's Plays, Hamlet to The Tempest* (New York: Routledge, 1992), 158.

19 Thomas Sorge, 'The Failure of Orthodoxy in *Coriolanus*' in *Shakespeare Reproduced: The Text in History and Ideology*, ed. Jean E. Howard and Marion F. O'Connor (New York: Methuen, 1987), 225–41 (237).

him by withdrawing her support – 'Do as thou list' (3.2.128) – and he
is childishly contrite:

> Mother, I am going to the market-place.
> Chide me no more […]
> Look, I am going
>
> (3.2.131–2, 134)

I see the dislocation in their relationship as a direct result of Volumnia's
determination to crown her old age with her son's glory which leads to
Coriolanus' severance from Rome and his eventual death. Her ambitions
also undermine her own self-assurance. Because she attempts to change
her son's nature by changing her own she is left more vulnerable than
he is when all comes to grief. Coriolanus has at least stuck to his guns
but Volumnia has forfeited her old strength and standing, and not only
in her son's eyes. We are aware of a new carefulness in her as she urges
her departing son, 'Determine on some course / More than a wild
exposure to each chance […]' (4.1.36–7). Coriolanus would like the old,
tough mother back, 'Where is your ancient courage?' (4.1.3) but when
he goes he lumps Volumnia in with the others – Virgilia, Memenius
and Cominius – who are variously drooping and weeping. I see this as
a crucial moment for Volumnia. She is not seeing her son off to a 'cruel
war' (1.3.13) and the anticipated glories which have sustained, even
justified, her own existence. This is her son's dismissal and disgrace and
it renders her weak and inarticulate. Her subsequent confrontation with
the tribunes, discussed earlier, has only a faint echo of her old spirit and
this is collapsed by what is easily identified by the men as the stereotypical
ranting of a foolish and ageing female. Almost too tearful to make them
understand her feelings she is soon incoherent – 'If that I could for
weeping, you should hear–/ Nay, and you shall hear some', 'I'll tell thee
what – yet go. / Nay but thou shalt stay too' (4.2.15–16, 24–5).

When Coriolanus joins with Rome's enemies to attack the city it is
a different Volumnia, ageing and pitiable, who goes to plead with her
son. She still tries to manipulate him – 'thou art my warrior. / I holp to
frame thee' (5.3.62–3) – but her old assurance has gone and she places

herself as a stereotypical old mother, no longer masculine and strong but female and helpless, fearful of losing 'The country, our dear nurse, or else thy person, / Our comfort in the country' (5.3.111–12). Her language becomes domestic, diminished and self-pitying:

> Thou hast never in thy life
> Showed thy dear mother any courtesy,
> When she, poor hen, fond of no second brood,
> Has clucked thee to the wars and safely home
>
> (5.3.161–4)

Again she urges political compromise upon him and this time she prevails.

Much has been made of the moment when Coriolanus gives way to his mother and the linked stage direction, *he holds her by the hand, silent*. This can be seen as Coriolanus becoming 'a child again',[20] or evidence that Volumnia has so dismantled her son as to reduce him to 'a womanly silence'.[21] Again, though, Volumnia's age is not taken into account yet this is apparent in her helpless and pathetic final words:

> I am hushed until our city be afire,
> And then I'll speak a little.
>
> (5.3.182–3)

At this point a son might well take his mother's hand, motivated not by a return to childhood but by mature sympathy for an old woman whose helplessness has succeeded in winning him over but who doesn't recognise the awful significance of her successful pleading – 'The gods look down and this unnatural scene / They laugh at' (5.3.185–6).

We do not know if Volumnia becomes aware of the 'unnatural' thing she has done as Shakespeare gives us no further insight into

---

20 Adelman, 161.
21 Sorge, 237.

her feelings. She is feted in procession as the saviour of Rome in Act 5 scene 5 but does not speak again. Her initial masculine strength has gone and in old age her once assertive language is finally reduced to 'appropriate' female silence.

'Egypt's Widow'

While Shakespeare's Antony is usually presented on stage as an ageing man, to accentuate the collapse of his military and political powers and provide a splendid role for the more mature male actor, his 'serpent of old Nile' (1.5.25) has not always been taken at her word as being 'wrinkled deep in time' (1.5.29). So it's encouraging that recent productions have gained from our now living in 'a time of increased longevity and interest in aging' which allows emphasis on the play 'as a drama of middle-age love'.[22] For there's no doubt that Shakespeare's text powerfully explores Cleopatra's genuine anxieties about the fact that she's ageing, setting her vanity alongside trepidation about the possible waning of her sexual powers and showing the importance of these matters to herself and her country. He does this by presenting the stereotype of the lust-driven older woman fearful of losing her sexual attraction and then boldly subverting this stereotype. He also gives his Queen language which reveals her ability to conform to appropriate female behaviour and at the same time defiantly sweep this aside. It's good to see these age-related issues more fully engaged with on the modern stage.

In Part 1 of this book I refer to the ageing of Queen Elizabeth and how this influenced the way she presented herself to public view, in terms of real and sexual politics, and Shakespeare's characterisation of Cleopatra encompasses this aspect of female rule. It's not surprising that 'many parallels between the two canny and calculating queens' are acknowledged.[23] For Egypt's Queen the apparently self-congratulatory acceptance of wrinkles is speedily undermined by the unexpected news

---

22 Sara Munson Deats, *Antony and Cleopatra New Critical Essays* (Abingdon: Routledge, 2005), 79.
23 Ibid., 24.

---

of Antony's remarriage to the younger Octavia. Cleopatra responds to this with a ferocious physical attack on the hapless messenger who brings the information, beating him up, drawing a knife on him and threatening torture – 'Thou shalt be whipped with wire and stewed in brine' (2.5.64). But her desperate cry, 'Rogue, thou hast lived too long' (2.5.73), though directed at the messenger, reflects her more realistic acknowledgement of her own age. Her rage and confusion in this scene carry great dramatic power but, of course, undermine royal dignity. This treatment of the character is completely opposite to that of Samuel Daniel in *The Tragedy of Cleopatra* (1594). His Queen meditates more soberly upon her situation, presenting herself as Antony's 'debtor' because he gave up so much for a woman past her best. She considers her age and lost looks in elegiac form:

> And yet thou came'st but in my beauty's wane,
> When new appearing wrinkles of declining
> Wrought with the hand of years, seemed to detain
> My grace's light, as now but dimly shining,
> Even in the confines of mine age
>
> (1.171–5)

The calm acceptance by an ageing woman of 'this Autumn of my beauty' (1.181) is confirmed as appropriate behaviour through the dignity of the language. By contrast the loss of self-control in Shakespeare's Cleopatra is cause for discomfort in all who witness it. The battered messenger takes to his heels; Charmian urges restraint upon her mistress – 'keep yourself within yourself' (2.5.65); and of course the audience is made equally uneasy by the older woman's lack of restraint. Yet the hysterical response of this Cleopatra reflects far more forcibly female fears about ageing and its consequences.

However, Shakespeare doesn't leave this issue with a stereotypical image of the jealous, scared, over-excited older woman. Cleopatra's later questioning of the messenger in Act 3 scene 3 is calmer and more measured and initially focuses on the self-presentation of Antony's new bride – 'Dull of tongue, and dwarfish [...] There's nothing in her yet' (3.3.16, 23).

But her response to the messenger's revelation of Octavia's age – '[…] I do think she's thirty' (3.3.28) – is a sharp question about the woman's looks – 'Bear'st thou her face in mind? Is't long or round?' (3.3.29). She does not want to dwell on the age difference, once this is revealed, but seeks reassurance that her own looks and sexual attraction are superior to those of Octavia. This is crucial to her for although we have Enobarbus' assertion that 'Age cannot wither her' (2.2.241), Shakespeare makes it clear that this old soldier's remarkably lyrical description of the way Cleopatra 'pursed up' (2.2.193–4) Antony's heart at Cydnus relates to the start of their relationship. When the play opens they have been together for some time and have had a number of children. And although Enobarbus observes that she 'makes hungry / Where most she satisfies' (2.2.243–4) providing an image of Cleopatra as an eternal, entrancing, sex-fantasy object for all men, Shakespeare shows that in reality her sexuality now centres solely upon Antony. When she recalls her earlier affair with Caesar she places it firmly in the past – 'When I was green in judgement, cold in blood' (1.5.73). Her present is entirely occupied by Antony and all past actions judged against her behaviour with him – 'Did I, Charmian, / Ever use Caesar so?' (1.5.65–6). Cleopatra is not coquettishly tallying up conquests here but reflecting on youthful love and comparing this with her present, mature relationship. There may have been other loves in her life but Antony is now her only focus, her 'man of men' (1.5.71).

It's clear, too, that this passionate partnership has also worn into a companionable relationship. Philo's salacious opening comments about Antony's sexual enthralment to Cleopatra dismiss him as 'a strumpet's fool' (1.1.13). But very soon after this we learn that what the mature couple actually have planned for tonight is an outing 'to wander through the streets and note / The qualities of people' (1.1.55–6). Cleopatra's reminiscences of exciting times with Antony include fishing trips, all-night drinking bouts and cross-dressing romps (2.5) and, while such activities need not preclude sex of the most inventive and satisfying kind, the image of this couple is that of companions in pleasures which aren't always sexual. That Cleopatra's first wild response to the news of Antony's marriage is followed by probing questions reveals the acute consternation of an ageing woman who has lived with her lover for years and is suddenly facing a rival who is younger and potentially more sexually attractive. Though she welcomes them, the messenger's revised responses, now thoroughly well-judged, do not truly reassure her as the uncertainty of her final, halting remark makes clear – 'All may be well enough' (3.3.46).

Shakespeare opens up the panic experienced in this situation even by a woman whose physical attractions are confirmed as timeless by male observation. But he also emphasises the problematic political situation which will arise if Cleopatra has indeed lost her Antony. When Alexas flatteringly justifies the messenger's fear by saying that even 'Herod of Jewry' (a name with grim New Testament connections for a contemporary audience) could not face an irate Cleopatra, the Queen boastfully asserts 'That Herod's head I'll have'. She then has to acknowledge the limitations of her power – 'but how, when Antony is gone, / Through whom I might command it?' (3.3.3, 4–5, 5–6). Her own political position and influence are entirely dependent upon continuing support from her lover.

Like Fletcher's Bonduca, Shakespeare's Queen also understands the importance of the way language is used but Cleopatra has achieved far greater facility here and is always aware of what words can conceal and reveal. This is seen in her initial exchange with the messenger as, fearful about the news he brings, she picks at almost every utterance:

> **Messenger.** First madam, he is well
> **Cleopatra.** [...] we use
> To say the dead are well [...]
> **Messenger.** But yet, madam –
> **Cleopatra.** I do not like 'But yet'; it does allay
> The good precedence.
> (2.5.30–32, 49–51)

Similarly, when Thidius lays out for her the terms which will allow her to repudiate her relationship with Antony she doesn't miss his reference to Caesar's protection as a 'shroud' and she refers to Egypt's 'doom' in her flowery and ingratiating response (3.13.71, 78). Thidius isn't sharp enough to realise that her obsequious words of apparent agreement – 'I kiss his conquering hand. Tell him I am prompt / To lay my crown at's feet' (3.13.75–6) – in fact shroud a refusal. She too is Egypt: she lays down her own crown and hears her own doom because she will not give up Antony. And this almost superstitious reliance on the power of language is most obvious when Antony is dying, for she tries to use speech to hold off the inevitable, picturing herself as controlling fate in this way – 'let me rail so high / That the false hussy Fortune break her wheel' (4.16.45–6). Even in her angry response to Caesar's renewed overtures, 'He words me girls', we see the recognition of one skilled speaker by another (5.2.187).

Certainly Cleopatra maintains Antony's focus upon her by using language that is witty, direct, over-emphatic, often self-pitying, and by spinning words cleverly to hold his attention. This is demonstrated right at the start of the play when she turns the interruption from Rome to her own advantage by talking Antony out of seeing the newly arrived messengers. It is he who has all the beautiful language here as he confirms his love for her – 'Now, for the love of Love and her soft hours / Let's not confound the time with conference harsh' (1.1.46–7). Even his 'wrangling queen' admonition (1.1.50) is qualified by tenderness. Her speech, on the other hand, is brisk, mocking and direct, delivered in a clipped and aggressive style as she urges him to listen to the latest information from Rome – 'Nay, hear them, Antony. / Fulvia perchance is angry [...] Nay, and most like / You must not stay here longer' (1.1.20–21; 27–8). Yet the end result of her 'wrangling' is that the messengers are spurned and she takes Antony away with her. Of course he receives the news eventually but for now, in public and before her court and his friends, it is Cleopatra's 'messenger' (1.1.54) who has his exclusive attention. But Cleopatra's use of language for such manipulative purposes is not just a politician's public gimmick. Their confrontation in relative privacy, when Antony is leaving for Rome, sees her scolding and ranting and deliberately becoming so uncontrollable that Antony can't get a word in edgeways. Despite the apparent hysteria her words are chosen for maximum effect to show him how much he is hurting her – she is 'mightily betrayed!' (1.3.25) and, though aggressively couched, her reference to the 'heart in Egypt' (1.3.41) acts as a prompt for Antony's reassurance that his 'full heart' (1.3.43) is still hers, whatever the changing political situation.

However, Shakespeare shows that even a woman as skilled in use of language as this can fall victim to the garrulousness of age, lacking full control over her tongue. Having achieved confirmation of Antony's continuing commitment to her in Act 1 scene 3 – vital to her political and personal survival – it is ill-judged of Cleopatra to begin a second sharp-worded attack when Fulvia's death is mentioned. Maybe she is genuinely taken aback by Antony's callous comment on this news, 'At the last, best' (1.3.61). At all events she allows her language to become so provocative and mocking that Antony closes down into cold courtesy – 'I'll leave you lady' (1.3.86) – making it clear she has gone too far. She has the wit and sensitivity to recognise this and retrieve the situation by allowing her own words to falter:

> Courteous lord, one word.
> Sir, you and I must part; but that's not it.
> Sir, you and I have loved; but there's not it.
> That you know well. Something it is I would –
> O, my oblivion is a very Antony,
>
> (1.3.87–91)

The result is an image of a garrulous woman suddenly and vulnerably seeking for appropriate words of appeasement. Antony's response is one of fond exasperation (1.3.92) and the situation is saved. A similar lack of control in Cleopatra appears when the dying Antony is carried to her monument. Protesting that she dare not set foot outside she presents herself as safe there from both Caesar and 'Your wife Octavia with her modest eyes / And still conclusion' (4.16.28–9). It seems extraordinary that she should still be getting at Antony about his marriage at such a time. Again, though, she retrieves the awkward moment – here with the 'sport' (4.16.331) of drawing Antony up to her. These episodes serve to emphasise Shakespeare's use and subversion of the image of a verbose ageing woman. The tension created by Cleopatra's inability to control her tongue is then defused by her quick use of that tongue, and the stereotype is overturned so we see a woman skilful in adapting her language whenever necessary.

Even when she is apparently wrong-footed Cleopatra can access the right words, as when Antony rants at her apparent warmth towards Thidius. Though seemingly reduced almost to monosyllables by his fury, she eventually calms him with a soothing and appeasing refutation of his suspicions that she is 'Cold-hearted' (3.13.161) towards him:

> Ah, dear, if I be so
> From my cold heart let heaven engender hail,
> And poison it in the source, and the first stone
> Drop in my neck: as it determines, so
> Dissolve my life!
>
> (3.13.161–5)

Similarly, when she is blamed for Antony's military errors in the debacle of the first sea-fight she doesn't attempt to talk or argue her way out of the situation but uses simple apology – 'Forgive my fearful sails!'; 'O, my pardon!'; 'Pardon, pardon!' (3.11.55, 61, 68). This wins over her lover almost at once and he urges, 'Fall not a tear, I say. One of them rates / All that is won and lost' (3.11.69–70). The positive response elicited in each case confirms the appropriateness of her tactful and self-deprecating language. When she wants to Cleopatra can lay tongue to the right words and we see her mollifying the conquering Caesar with similarly appropriate female language, confessing the 'frailties which before / Have often shamed our sex' (5.2.119–20). Here, when it's revealed that she has been salting away some of her assets, she creates an image of herself as ill-served by her treasurer and embarrassingly caught out by his audit, interested only in frivolous 'lady trifles' and generally 'to be pitied' (5.2.161, 175). Caesar is entirely taken in by all this verbal triviality, assuring her of his 'care and pity' (5.2.184), and so, unwittingly, gives her the opportunity to plan and carry out her suicide.

The only time Cleopatra's clever and complex speech patterns completely collapse is after the moving domestic moments when she helps Antony arm himself for the coming battle and he parts from her with 'a soldier's kiss' (4.4.30). Left with only Charmian Cleopatra's previous upbeat mood swiftly dissolves. 'He goes forth gallantly' (4.4.36) is positive enough, but her final line, 'Then, Antony - but now. Well, on' (4.4.38) is fractured and almost incoherent. At this time of private despair she is, uniquely, lost for words.

Like Bonduca, Cleopatra chooses to kill herself rather than submit to Roman rule, acknowledging her value as a trophy and sharing her fears with her women – 'I shall see / Some squeaking Cleopatra boy my greatness' (5.2.215–16). But this is a private defiance in contrast to the public declarations made, from the battlements of her fort, by Fletcher's Queen. However, because Shakespeare places Cleopatra's suicide at the end of the play, the final action of which is the removal of her body, her death remains with the audience as Bonduca's does not. It's also worth noting that while Bonduca's daughters die with her they are nagged and coerced into this. By contrast Cleopatra does not directly influence the choice of Iras and Charmian to die with their mistress so the fact that they do so voluntarily enhances our picture of a woman who inspires remarkable loyalty in her attendants.

While it's not unusual for characters on the Early Modern stage to speak as they die – and often at surprising length, given the circumstances – Shakespeare's intense focus upon Cleopatra's language at this point not only ensures our total engagement with her actions but maintains her presence after her death. Her calm responses to the Clown who smuggles in the poisonous asps, the means of her suicide, suggest the quiet amusement of a woman at ease with herself. Yet there is no abandoning of her state and her insistence upon being dressed in her robes and regalia reflects her sense that she is engaged in a momentous undertaking, one which Antony will approve of as honourable – 'I see him rouse himself / To praise my noble act' (5.2.279–80). However, she is not going passively to her death and the wit and facility with words that have marked her out in life are not lost. When Iras dies before her Cleopatra sensually portrays death as 'a lover's pinch / Which hurts and is desired', while urging herself on in case her servant should receive Antony's welcoming kiss, 'Which is my heaven to have' (5.2.290–91, 298). Even as the asp does its work she is sharply mocking of Caesar as an 'ass / Unpolicied' (5.2.302–3). She remains remarkable with her final, ironically feminine image of herself as a young mother – 'Dost thou not see my baby at my breast, / That sucks the nurse asleep?' (5.2.304–5). We have had no cause to consider Cleopatra's maternal attributes in this play but at the moment of her death she wittily uses the means of that death to create another dramatic role for herself. The words finally run out – 'What should I stay—' (5.2.308) – but it is telling that she should die in mid-sentence, vocal to the last.

Cleopatra's death is so memorable that it conflicts with and defeats male attempts to diminish her actions. Her body, in all its costumed glory, remains before the audience as Caesar attempts to reduce the political and emotional impact of what she has done. Initially, his words seem positive as he refers to the way in which death has not undermined the Queen's physical attractions. He images her as able still to 'catch another Antony / In her strong toil of grace' (5.2.341–2). Yet his language and his insistence upon her being buried with Antony, creating a picture of this 'pair so famous' (5.2.354) clasped together for eternity in their shared grave, serve to maintain the reductive stereotype of Cleopatra as a lustful gypsy portrayed in the play's first scene. His term 'noble weakness' (5.2.338) warns that her suicide ought not to be viewed in the same way as Antony's and his description of her seeking 'easy ways to die' (5.2.350) tries to reduce Cleopatra's suicide to something less admirable than that of her lover. In death she should be subsumed into Antony, and Caesar insists it is 'his glory which / Brought them to be lamented' (5.2.366–7). However, the presence of Cleopatra's robed body on stage as he speaks, coupled with the recent memory of her rich linguistic approach to death entirely subvert any attempt to reduce the powerful impact of that death. I think there is a wry nod towards dramatic convention in the fact that when preparing for her suicide 'Egypt's widow' acknowledges what is expected of all 'good' widows and looks to embrace the married state with Antony – 'Husband, I come' (5.2.282).

Part IV

PAULINA'S POWER

The power of Paulina in *The Winter's Tale* is related in part to the way she speaks out in public, in defence of the wronged Queen Hermione. This makes her the focus of principled action through the play and has nothing to do with her domestic roles as wife to Antigonus, one of the King's counsellors, as mother to their children and later as his widow. But her power is also seen in the way she creates, directs and performs in the drama of Act 5 which restores the royal marriage and enables the reconciliation of all affected by its rupture. Shakespeare refers to the standard old woman stereotype in presenting Paulina as garrulous – she is criticised as being 'Of boundless tongue', (2.3. 91–2) – but it is telling that of all the old women in Early Modern drama only Paulina is still vocal and still alive at the end of a play which owes its conclusion to her authorial creativity. Although she is in danger of being reclaimed for control by patriarchal rules at the conclusion, when a remarriage is mooted, the central male character, King Leontes, acknowledges Paulina's on-going power and influence. Shakespeare's own acknowledgement of the continuing importance of the older woman in contemporary society is unequivocal in this instance.

From her first appearance, after Hermione has been imprisoned by Leontes for supposed adultery, Paulina is shown as a manipulator – not only of the situation but of the men she is dealing with – and while her manipulative skills are initially undermined by stereotypical garrulousness we see her becoming increasingly confident in her use of language as a tool for direction and control.

Her bossy behaviour at the prison – 'The keeper of the prison, call to him / Let him have knowledge who I am' (2.2.1–2) – and her annoyance at being refused access to Hermione as well as her domineering attitude overall, imply that Paulina is just a typically talkative older woman who tries to get her own way by being loud and aggressive. Equally, her sweeping reassurance to the jailer, 'Do not you fear. Upon mine honour, / I will stand twixt you and danger' (2.2.68–9), seems the boasting of someone full of her own importance. Shakespeare subverts the stereotypes though by showing that Paulina's manipulative powers actually get her the information she needs. More importantly she recognises the potential power of her own language to help Hermione:

> I'll use that tongue I have. If wit flow from't
> As boldness from my bosom, let't not be doubted
> I shall do good.
>
> (2.2.55–7)

Paulina's maturity gives her that 'boldness' which is necessary in standing up to a monarch who is also a jealous husband. Indeed she sees this as a duty – 'These dangerous, unsafe lunes i'th' King, beshrew them! / He must be told on't, and he shall' (2.2.33–4). When she confronts Leontes she shows some tact in presenting her words as 'medicinal' (2.3.37) and herself as a mother figure or caring nurse to the King, one who has 'come to bring him sleep' and 'purge him of that humour / That presses him' (2.3.33, 38–9). Yet she has already decided against being 'honey-tongued' (2.2.36) and is determined to force Leontes into accepting the truth that Hermione is faithful and their new-born child legitimate. She certainly won't 'creep like shadows by him' as the other courtiers are doing (2.3.34). So, 'the lines of battle are clearly drawn between two kinds of power: Paulina's female tongue versus Leontes' masculine rule'.[1]

Her subsequent reference to 'some gossips for your highness' (2.3.41) is unfortunate. Paulina is referring to the need for choosing godparents for the new baby but gossip has a different connotation for Leontes at the moment. He is obsessed with being talked of as

---

1 Patricia Southard Gourley, '"O my most sacred lady": Female Metaphor in *The Winter's Tale*' in *The Winter's Tale Critical Essays*, ed. Maurice Hunt (London: Garland Publishing, 1995), 258–79 (265).

a cuckold – 'They're here with me already, whisp'ring, rounding' (1.2.217–18). However, the words shake him out of his unhealthy brooding and he turns on this 'audacious lady!' (2.3.42). His angry mocking of Antigonus as another put-upon husband, 'What, canst not rule her?' enables Paulina to open her argument – 'From all dishonesty he can' – and point up Leontes' error in imprisoning an honest wife (2.3.46, 47). Again she emphasises herself as the King's 'loyal servant [...] physician [...] obedient counsellor,' (2.3.54–5) but her language is too direct. Her announcement that she comes from Leontes' 'good queen' (2.3.58) results in his ordering of her ejection. The fierce conflict which follows distracts from our understanding that Paulina is morally correct. Leontes' actions are, indeed, 'dangerous, unsafe', and Shakespeare has already established that the men about the King are helpless to influence him, so that it's entirely appropriate for a strong-minded, mature woman of integrity to attempt 'the office' (2.2.34). Yet her shouting match with Leontes, her threats of physical violence to anyone who attempts to eject her – 'Let him that makes but trifles of his eyes / First hand me' (2.3.63) – and her defiance of her husband all undermine her true intentions and seem to show her as lacking in dignity and circumspection. Indeed her remarks about Leontes' 'weak-hinged fancy' (2.3.119) could be seen as 'emasculating' him 'by calling attention to his mental impotence'.[2] When she denounces him as a 'tyrant' and 'scandalous to the world' (2.3.116, 121) Leontes is able to dismiss her as an uncontrollable wife. His age-specific insults – 'witch', 'bawd', 'crone' 'gross hag' (2.3.69, 77, 108) – access the standard image of a mature woman lacking any mature self-control. This is reinforced by Antigonus' inability to 'stay her tongue' (2.3.11) and his seemingly feeble attitude to Paulina's defiance, 'When she will take the rein, I let her run; / But she'll not stumble' (2.3.51–2). This is an older wife who appears to have emasculated her husband! Shakespeare shows the sound intentions of this woman of integrity, who attempts to restore her King's sanity by

2 Michelle Ephraim, 'Hermione's Suspicious Body: Adultery and Superfetation in *The Winter's Tale*' in *Performing Maternity in Early Modern England*, ed. Kathryn M. Moncrief and Kathryn R. McPherson (Aldershot: Ashgate, 2007), 45–58 (55).

honest speaking, undermined by carefully targeted male aggression. However, it's clear that although she doesn't change the King's mind Paulina's influence does save Hermione's new-born daughter from being brained or burnt by Leontes (2.3.140–41).

Very speedily, though, Paulina acquires strict control of her own language in order to control the actions of others. And at the same time she uses the male-imposed stereotype of herself as a garrulous, interfering older woman to conceal her true intentions. In Act 3 scene 2 when Leontes defies the oracle who has confirmed his wife's innocence, he loses Hermione. It is Paulina who publicly and with exact detail catalogues his sins. Her words imply that she is completely overcome by grief – 'O, cut my lace, lest my heart cracking it, / Break too' (3.2.172–3) – but she is in full command of the situation as we see from her immediate reference to Leontes as a 'tyrant' and her taunting image of this 'tyranny' devising spectacular punishments for her truth-telling (3.2.174, 178). Like the King, we are reminded of his denial of Paulina's earlier charge of tyranny (2.3.120). Then he controlled the situation: now that control has shifted to Paulina who goes on to denounce him as 'a fool inconstant', a poisoner of honour, worse than a devil, 'a gross and foolish sire' (3.2.185, 191). Her revelation of Hermione's supposed death couples female tenderness with unbending outrage – 'the sweet'st, dear'st creature's dead, and vengeance for't / Not dropped down yet' (3.2.200–201). Her language is designed to divert possible suspicion. In the same way the manipulative nature of her next words – 'I say she's dead. I'll swear't' (3.2.202) – and her defying her listeners to restore the Queen forces their acceptance of the death. Leontes certainly has no doubts, allowing Paulina to continue her castigation of him, this time in terms of the impossibility of his ever doing penance enough. Although what she says is just and welcomed by the guilty Leontes himself – 'Go on, go on: / Thou canst not speak too much' (3.2.213–14) – it's clear that her manner is considered unsuitable by her other male listeners, for she is warned for the 'boldness' of her speech and told to be quiet (3.2.217). Still playing the outspoken old woman she apologises, wordily, and emphasises her 'rashness' (3.2.220) only to then extend that rashness and, as 'a foolish woman' (3.2.226) revisit all the areas most painful for Leontes:

> The love I bore your queen — lo, fool again!
> I'll speak of her no more [...]
> I'll not remember you of my own lord,
> Who is lost too
>
> (3.2.227–30)

In referring to herself as rash and foolish even as she continues to speak out in rashness and folly, Paulina seems to underline the faults of the garrulous ageing female, while in fact emphasising the crimes Leontes has committed and so manipulating his response which acknowledges those crimes:

> Thou didst speak but well
> When most the truth, which I receive much better
> Than to be pitied of thee.
>
> (3.2.231–3)

Paulina has taken control of Hermione's death and Leontes' response to it by utilising the seemingly uncontrollable loquacity of the older woman.

When we next see Paulina, 16 years on, she is still manipulating Leontes with constant reminders of his past errors. Though he promised daily acts of repentance (3.2.237–41) there was no mention of a role for Paulina at that time. So it is evidence of her influence that she has established herself as keeper of the King's conscience. This she regularly pricks with painful recollections of Hermione which he finds no easier to bear with the passage of time:

> Killed?,
> She I killed? I did so [...]
> Now, good now,
> Say so but seldom.
>
> (5.1.16–17)

His courtiers resent Paulina's interference in the politically sensitive issue of his possible remarriage but again she utilises the stereotypical behaviour of old women in harking back to the past to encourage Leontes to set aside concerns about the future. She refers to the oracle's ruling that 'King Leontes shall not have an heir / Till his lost child be found...' and urges him, 'Care not for issue, / The crown will find an heir' (5.1.46–7), to ensure his continuing foregrounding of the memory of Hermione. This enables her to maintain control of the King, extracting a promise that he will only remarry with her approval and he acknowledges her right to do so:

> O, that ever I
> Had squared me to thy counsel! Then even now
> I might have looked upon my queen's full eyes,
> Have taken treasure from her lips.
>
> (5.1.51–4)

Paulina's dogged refusal to bury the past is imaged as part of Leontes' punishment but can be seen as positive, stimulating 'the shame which is necessary for rebuilding basic concepts'.[3] But Shakespeare is also engaging here with the tension between the need for remembrance of things past as essential to the process of rediscovery and reconciliation (and, of course, to the development of the plot), and natural human discomfort at the tendency of the ageing remembrancer to be so frequently outspoken.

That Paulina's 'boundless tongue' has enabled her to control events becomes apparent in the play's final scene when she uses it to draw all concerned into the magic that is Hermione's restoration. In doing so she becomes a female play-maker and director, organising the action and manipulating the responses of her performers who are also her audience. Added to this she is a performer herself in the drama she

---

3 Eugene England, 'Cordelia and Paulina, Shakespeare's Healing Dramatists', in *Literature and Belief* 2 (1982), 69–82 (79).

has devised, playing the crucial role of magician and controller of the denouement.

Leontes, released from a measure of guilt by the restoration of his lost daughter Perdita, publicly recognises the 'grave and good' Paulina who has given him 'great comfort' (5.3.1). She confirms that her manipulation of events has been honestly meant – 'What, sovereign sir, / I did not well, I meant well' (5.3.2–3). Now she abandons the loud and challenging tones of the verbose old woman and her language becomes increasingly soft and hypnotic as she reveals the 'newly performed' statue of Hermione (5.2.95). Her manipulation now is that of a playwright who can alter time, for when Leontes exclaims at Hermione's wrinkles Paulina has an explanation – 'So much the more our carver's excellence / Which lets go by some sixteen years, and makes her / As she lived now' (5.3.30–32). She encourages her audience, on stage and beyond, to believe in the fabrication – 'your fancy / May think anon it moves', 'My lord's almost so far transported that / He'll think anon it lives' (5.3.60–61; 69–70) – while reinforcing their need for that belief by threatening to close down the show – 'No longer shall you gaze on't […] I'll draw the curtain' (5.3.60, 68). At their protests she tantalises them by offering greater, forbidden delights – 'I could afflict you farther' (5.3.75). It is not only the statue but Paulina's performance which is 'Masterly done' (5.3.65).

When she offers to make the statue of Hermione move her calm, directorial authority takes on a religious quality – 'It is required / You do awake your faith' (5.3.94–5) – and she takes total control of the situation. She cues the music, directs Hermione's action – ''Tis time. Descend. Be stone no more' (5.3.99) – and instructs Leontes in how he must react – 'Start not', 'present your hand' (5.3.104, 107). She also contains the responses of other characters in the drama – 'Mark a little while' (5.3.119) – and places Perdita appropriately to 'pray your mother's blessing' (5.3.121). Paulina's play is performed exactly as she wishes and the result is reconciliation and concord.

It must be said that Paulina is not the only mature female character seen on stage as a director of drama. In George Peele's

The Old Wives' Tale (1590) Madge, the old wife in question, becomes the playwright's substitute on stage and this play is unique in having a woman as narrator. Again we see the playwright initially drawing on stereotypical images, this time of the caring, ageing female, in establishing this character. Three pages lost in a wood are given shelter by Madge and her husband and offered food – 'a piece of cheese and pudding of my own making' (61–2) – and there is confirmation of the old woman's sound behaviour and attitudes when she is praised as 'a good example for the wives of our town' (63–4) by one of the guests. That such a proper old party will have a collection of tales to tell to entertain the unexpected visitors is taken for granted by Frolic – 'I am sure you are not without a score' (87) – and Fantastic considers such stories ideal refreshment (88–9). Madge duly agrees to provide entertainment while her husband goes off to bed. Her comment 'they that ply their work must keep good hours' (95–6) indicates that she is dutifully attendant to her man's physical requirements.

Peele's subsequent handling of Madge reveals a character capable of accessing a range of linguistic styles. As the play begins her language takes on a lyrical quality for her introduction of the 'fair daughter' who is 'as white as snow, and as red as blood' (114–15). However, she smartly and coarsely closes down any logical objections to a fantastic story when she tells her listeners 'either hear my tale, or kiss my tail' (120). The narrative is not smoothly achieved for Madge, as an impromptu storyteller, is putting the tale together as she goes along, running ahead of herself on occasions and then having to insert characters and actions she has left out:

> O Lord I quite forgot, there was a Conjurer [...]
> O I forget! She (he I would say) turned a proper young
> man to a bear in the night, and a man in the day, and
> keeps by a cross that parts three several ways, and
> he made his lady run mad. Gods me bones! who comes here?
>
> (122, 128–32)

She is also comically long-winded, disrupting the narrative flow with inconsequential chatter:

> this is he; and this man that came to him
> was a beggar, and dwelt upon a green. But soft, who comes here? O
> these are the harvest men; ten to one they sing a song of mowing.
>
> (256–9)

But because she *is* the narrator all this gives a fascinating insight into how the author of such a text handles plot development, clarifies aspects of story and character, and has to bow to audience expectation in relation to some characters. She directs the action of the performers, highlighting the song of the harvest men, explaining the characters' behaviour and filling in necessary back-story. We also see examples of Madge's creative involvement in the play through her intervention – 'this is one that is going to the conjurer' (266). Certainly her discussion of characters is designed to encourage response – 'O, this Jack was a marvellous fellow. / He was but a poor man, but very well beloved' (556–7).

But this active involvement in storytelling doesn't last. Peele silences Madge part-way through the play within a play and we find that at the end she has fallen asleep over her own story, thus surrendering the role of narrator to the playwright. Madge is now shifted back into being simply a home-maker and provider – 'Let us in. We will have a cup of ale' (964). In denying the character final centrality Peele appears to endorse the containment of the old woman within the domestic sphere, caring for husband and guests and limiting any storytelling to the realms of home and private entertainment. However, this doesn't negate the fact that it is Madge's speaking which releases the magic of the tale.

Shakespeare, though, achieves much more. He shows in Paulina a mature woman using and subverting the stereotypes placed on her age and gender by her society to achieve the kind of control no such woman should even admit to desiring, let alone possess, and wielding it with admirable integrity. Having presented his audience with such images – every bit as remarkable as a statue coming to life – he then tantalises by threatening their removal. For it now seems that Paulina must forfeit the independence and autonomy she has acquired and resume the role of the mature widow who must remarry. It can be seen as inevitable for the restoration of male control that 'Paulina take a new mate who will rule her' because the hierarchy has been reversed by 'Leontes' sickness and Paulina's wisdom'.[4] It seems, too, that Leontes is reverting to and rewarding controlling behaviour in matching her with Camillo, who demonstrated greater strength of character than Antigonus in his earlier defiance of the then tyrannical king. The implication is that Camillo will hardly allow Paulina to 'take the rein' (2.3.51). So, in marrying this older widow off to an 'honourable husband' already prepared for the role – 'I partly know his mind' (5.3.144, 143) – Leontes seemingly enacts the silencing of a garrulous old woman – 'O peace, Paulina!' (5.3.136). It appears, too, that this play will conform to other 'romantic comedies' in which 'the transfer of power into the hands of women is temporary; it is always restored to the patriarchy'.[5] However, it's important to acknowledge that neither Paulina nor Camillo respond to the matchmaker's plans, a silence which is perhaps more than just a 'nod to the scepticism of the more judicious playgoers'.[6]

Yet Shakespeare wittily offers 'more amazement' (5.3.87) with regard to Paulina, the mature woman of 'worth and honesty' (5.3.145), by having Leontes confirm that she still occupies a position from which she will guide others – 'Good Paulina, / Lead us from hence' (5.3.152–3). I believe that, given his unconventional handling of Paulina's character, the dramatist deliberately leaves the issue

4 Dorothea Kehler, 'Shakespeare's Emilies and the Politics of Celibacy', in *In Another Country: Feminist Perspectives on Renaissance Drama*, ed. Dorothea Kehler and Susan Barker (Metuchen, NJ: The Scarecrow Press, 1991), 157–78 (165).
5 David Schalkwyk, '"A Lady's 'Verily' is as Potent as a Lord's": Women, Word and Witchcraft in *The Winter's Tale*', *English Literary Renaissance* 22 (1992): 242–72 (259).
6 Dorothea Faith Kehler, 'Shakespeare's Widows of a Certain Age: Celibacy and Economics', *MHRA Working Papers in the Humanities* 1 (2006): 17–30 (27).

of her being silenced and controlled by marriage open to question. Although Leontes is clearly in charge again, now that his sanity and balance are restored, his words indicate that he has no intention of losing the good influence and leadership, the 'worth and honesty' (5.3.145), of Paulina. She achieves dramatic autonomy through the refusal of her creator to maintain a stereotypical approach to the character, an autonomy which does not diminish as the play closes and Leontes urges, 'Good Paulina [...] Hastily lead away' (5.3.152, 156).

CONCLUSION

Although 'it was in the players' interests to please as many of the paying customers as they could, the women no less than the men'[1] it's clear from the material I've discussed here that not all female customers would see themselves presented in pleasing ways on stage in Shakespeare's day. The older woman would observe an emphasis on her potential for disobedience and disorder and the need to contain and control her. She would discern distinct stereotyping of 'good' and 'bad' behaviour and see her stage counterpart steered towards patterns of thought and action deemed appropriate by the patriarchal society she inhabited. Any evidence of the old woman experiencing sexual desire and seeking sexual satisfaction would bring on a massive increase in male mockery. Instead of being encouraged to value or even celebrate the ageing process she'd be urged to acknowledge changing physicality in negative terms, set against male standards of what was truly 'attractive'. It was the older woman's outspokenness which was presented as especially problematic – there was always the danger of her encouraging disobedience to, and subversion of, male governance. And the very fact of the older woman's loquacity was itself an uncomfortable and unavoidable reminder of male inability to silence the female tongue.

However, there was some reassurance for the old woman conveyed through the drama of the day. The constant dramatized reminders of this character's on-going involvement with the male-governed family implied that however old and ugly she became with advancing years, respect and security would be achieved if she maintained her place within such a family. Implicitly, the institution was seen as the means of controlling her potential for disorder, intemperance and disobedience. There would be

---

1 Phyllis Rackin, 'Mysogyny is Everywhere' in *A Feminist Companion to Shakespeare*, ed. Dympna Callaghan (Oxford: Blackwell, 1994), 53.

little or no reflection of the old woman's actual experiences outside the home (apart from the outrageous activities of the aged bawd). Certainly, no mention would be made of her active involvement in many areas of society as worker, carer, administrator, financier and so on. Only in the handful of plays by Shakespeare which I've discussed here would the ageing female theatre-goer see the stereotypes of ageing wives, mothers and widows overthrown and only in *The Winter's Tale* would she find confirmation of her power, autonomy and creativity.

How good it would be to end here, to embed this research in history. Sadly, it's also relevant to our own time where the representation of the ageing and old woman on stage, and now in film and television drama, is still limited and often stereotypical. Despite all we know now about the active lives of older women, even – indeed particularly – in their retirement years, in television drama older women are 'much less likely than older men to be portrayed as working outside the home' and are also imaged as 'significantly less successful than older men'.[2] Positive qualities in older women characters are deemed to be 'sweet, pleasant, giving and caring' while negative qualities are 'slow, feeble, cranky and repetitive'.[3] Researching a range of feature films and working in conjunction with the British Film Institute the Brent U3A (University of the Third Age) Film Group found that with few exceptions roles for older women 'do no justice to [their] lives and aspirations […] nor do they represent the contributions they make to society'. Brent members are still 'waiting for […] the film industry to discover the richness and diversity of older women's lives'.[4] Such limiting stereotypes affect the careers of actors who are women. In a 'Woman's Hour' discussion on BBC Radio 4 Jean Rogers, Vice President of Equity, pointed out that older women often get peripheral roles – 'The crime thriller is popular but there older women tend to be victims. Surely it is important that our culture represents our society?'[5] Just as in

---

2 Marlene Sanders, *Older Women and the Media* (United Nations Division for the Advancement of Women: 2002), 1.

3 Ibid., 2.

4 David Sharp and Sean Delaney, eds, *Older Women in Feature Films: A Research Guide About Representations of Women Over 60* (London: U3A and BFI, 2006), 3–4.

5 'Woman's Hour', May 2006. www.bbc.co.uk/radio4/womanshour/03/2006

Shakespeare's day, it's rare to find any kind of celebratory media vision of the ageing female body or of sexuality in the old woman. A survey by the now defunct UK Film Council reports that seven in ten women between the ages of 50 and 75 questioned felt their group was 'generally under-represented in films' and 61 per cent said 'women of their age were portrayed on the big screen as not having sexual needs or desires'.[6] In reference to the findings that 'cinema too often falls back on discredited stereotypes, including sexless older women',[7] the 'actress and cinemagoer' Harriet Walter, expressed frustration. 'In real life, women have never had such full diverse lives, nor kept their health, sex appeal and vitality for so long. It is discouraging that so few writers seem to portray this'.[8]

Given that certain attitudes towards the older woman seem not to have changed in over 400 years it's crucial to identify and expose such suppressive standardisation. Shakespeare did this with vigour and humour and, in his creation of Paulina, overthrew the stereotypes completely. While we await this positive process in twenty-first century drama it's encouraging to see older female actors pressing for dramatists to explore the positive aspects of being an old woman. It was the performance of Margaret Tyzack as Paulina in *The Winter's Tale* in 1980 which first brought home to me the exciting potential of this character. Sadly, Tyzack died while I was completing this book but two years ago she left on record her disquiet about the 'deeply insulting' way in which older women are portrayed in contemporary drama – 'If you watch TV or listen to the radio for a week, you would get the impression that everyone over the age of 60 has no control over their faculties'. She summed up the situation in a refreshingly crisp critique which Shakespeare might have relished – that a great deal of writing about older women was 'a load of clichéd old bollocks'.[9]

6 Ian J. Griffiths, 'Older Women Unhappy Over Portrayal in Films, Survey Shows', http://www.guardian.co.uk/film/2011/mar/28

7 Amelia Hill, 'Women, Gay and Black People Still Shown as Stereotypes in Film, Says Study', http://www.guardian.co.uk/film/2011/mar/18

8 Harriet Walter, 'Why Do Stories Never Involve Women Over 50?', http://www.guardian.co.uk/film/2011/mar/18

9 Lyn Gardner, 'Margaret Tyzack: The Accidental Actor', http://www.guardian.co.uk/stage/2009/jun/23/ Margaret-tyzack/print

BIBLIOGRAPHY

Plays

Anonymous. *A Warning For Fair Women* (1599)

Armin, Robert. *The Two Maids of Mortlake* (1608)

B. R. *Appius and Virginia* (1563)

Beaumont, Francis. *The Knight of the Burning Pestle* (1607)

Beaumont, Francis and John Fletcher. *The Woman Hater* (1606)

———. *A King and No King* (1611)

Chapman, George. *The Blind Beggar of Alexandria* (1596)

———. *An Humorous Day's Mirth* (1567)

———. *The Widow's Tears* (1605)

Chapman, George, Ben Jonson and John Marston. *Eastward Ho!* (1605)

Chettle, Henry. *The Tragedy of Hoffman* (1602)

Cooke, J. *Greene's Tu Quoque or The City Gallant* (1611)

Daniel, Samuel. *The Tragedy of Cleopatra* (1593)

———. *Hymen's Triumph* (1614)

Day, John. *The Isle of Gulls* (1606)

Dekker, Thomas. *The Shoemaker's Holiday or The Gentle Craft* (1599)

Dekker, Thomas and John Webster. *Westward Ho!* (1604)

Dekker, Thomas, John Day and William Haughton (attr.). *Lust's Dominion or The Lascivious Queen* (1600)

Field, Nathan. *A Woman Is a Weathercock* (1609)

Fletcher, John. *The Tamer Tamed* (1609–11)

———. *The Night Walker or The Little Thief* (1611)

———. *Bonduca* (1613)

———. *The Tragedy of Valentinian* (c.1614)

Fletcher, John, Francis Beaumont and Nathan Field (?). *Four Plays or Moral Representations in One: The Triumph of Love* (1612)

Greene, Robert. *Alphonsus King of Aragon* (1587)

———. *The Scottish History of James IV* (1590)

———. *Orlando Furioso* (1591)

Heywood, Thomas. *The First Part of King Edward the Fourth* (1599)

———. *The Wise Woman of Hoxton* (1604)

Jonson, Ben. *Cynthia's Revels* (1601)
———. *Sejanus His Fall* (1603)
———. *Cataline His Conspiracy* (1611)
———. *Bartholomew Fair* (1614)
Kyd, Thomas. *The Spanish Tragedy* (1587)
Lyly, John. *Sappho and Phao* (1584)
———. *Endymion* (1588)
———. *Mother Bombie* (1589)
Markham, Gervase and Lewis Machin. *The Dumb Knight* (1608)
Marlowe, Christopher. *The Massacre At Paris* (1593)
Marlowe, Christopher and Thomas Nashe. *Dido Queen of Carthage* (1587)
Marston, John. *Antonio's Revenge* (1600)
———. *The Malcontent* (1604)
———. *The Dutch Courtesan* (1604)
———. *Sophonisba* (1605)
Mason, John. *The Turk* (1607)
Middleton, Thomas. *A Mad World My Masters* (1604)
———. *The Phoenix* (1604)
———. *The Puritan or The Widow of Watling Street* (1606)
———. *The Revenger's Tragedy* (1606)
———. *Michaelmas Term* (1606)
———. *A Chaste Maid in Cheapside* (1611)
———. *No Wit, No Help Like a Woman's* (1613)
———. *The Witch* (1615)
Munday, Anthony. *John a Kent and John a Cumber* (1589)
Munday, Anthony and Henry Chettle. *The Downfall of Robert Earl of Huntingdon* (1598)
Peele, George. *The Old Wives' Tale* (1590)
———. *Edward I* (1591)
Phillips John. *The Play of Patient Grissil* (1559)
Porter, Henry. *The Two Angry Women of Abingdon* (1588)
Rowley, William. *A Shoe-Maker A Gentleman* (1608)
S. S. *The Honest Lawyer* (1615)
Shakespeare, William. *Titus Andronicus* (1592)
———. *The Comedy of Errors* (1594)
———. *Richard III* (1592–93)
———. *Romeo and Juliet* (1595)
———. *Richard II* (1595)
———. *King John* (1596)
———. *Henry IV Part 2* (1597)
———. *The Merry Wives of Windsor* (1597–98)

_____. *Hamlet* (1600–1601)

_____. *All's Well That Ends Well* (1606–1607)

_____. *Measure for Measure* (1604)

_____. *King Lear* (1605)

_____. *Pericles* (1607)

_____. *Antony and Cleopatra* (1607)

_____. *Coriolanus* (1608)

_____. *Cymbeline* (1609)

_____. *The Winter's Tale* (1610)

Shakespeare, William and John Fletcher. *Henry VIII* (1613)

Stevenson, William (?). *Gammer Gurton's Needle* (1553, published in 1575)

Webster, John. *The White Devil* (1612)

Editions

Anonymous. *A Warning For Fair Women*. Edited by Charles Dale Cannon. The Hague: Mouton, 1975.

Armin, Robert. *The Two Maids of Mortlake*. Edited by Alexander S. Liddie. New York: Garland Publishing, 1979.

Beaumont, Francis. *Dramatic Works in the Beaumont and Fletcher Canon*. 10 vols. Edited by Fredson Bowers. Cambridge: Cambridge University Press, 1966–96 (unless otherwise stated).

_____. *The Knight of the Burning Pestle*. In *The Revels Plays*, edited by Sheldon P. Zitner. Manchester: Manchester University Press, 1984.

Chapman, George. *An Humorous Day's Mirth, The Plays of George Chapman*. 2 vols. Edited by Allan Holaday. Cambridge: D. S. Brewer, 1987 (unless otherwise stated).

_____. *The Widow's Tears*. In *Regents Renaissance Drama Series*, edited by Ethel M. Smeak. London: Edward Arnold, 1997.

Chapman, George, Ben Jonson and John Marston. *Eastward Ho!* In *The Revels Plays*, edited by R. W. van Fossen. Manchester: Manchester University Press, 1979.

Chettle, Henry. *The Tragedy of Hoffman*. In *Malone Society Reprints*, edited by Harold Jenkins. Oxford: Oxford University Press, 1951 for 1950.

Cooke, J. *Greene's Tu Quoque or The City Gallant*. Edited by Alan J. Burman. New York: Garland Publishing, 1984.

Daniel, Samuel. *Hymen's Triumph; The Tragedy of Cleopatra*. In *Complete Works in Verse and Prose by Samuel Daniel*, edited by Alexander B. Grosart. New York: Russell and Russell, 1963.

Dekker, Thomas. *The Dramatic Works of Thomas Dekker*. 4 vols. Edited by Fredson Bowers. Cambridge: Cambridge University Press, 1955 (unless otherwise stated).

————. *The Wonderful Year and Selected Writings.* Edited by E. D. Pendry. London: Edward Arnold, 1969.

————. *The Shoemaker's Holiday or The Gentle Craft.* In *The Revels Plays*, edited by R. L. Smallwood and Stanley Wells. Manchester: Manchester University Press, 1979.

Field, Nathan. *A Woman Is a Weathercock.* In *The Plays of Nathan Field.* Edited by William Peery. Austin: University of Texas Press, 1950.

Fletcher, John. *Dramatic Works in the Beaumont and Fletcher Canon.* 10 vols. Edited by Fredson Bowers. Cambridge: Cambridge University Press 1966–96 (unless otherwise stated).

————. *The Tragedy of Valentinian.* In *Oxford English Drama*, edited by Martin Wiggins. Oxford: Oxford University Press, 1998.

Greene, Robert. *Alphonsus King of Aragon.* In *Malone Society Reprints*, edited by W. W. Greg. Oxford: Oxford University Press, 1926.

————. *Orlando Furioso.* In *Malone Society Reprints*, edited by W. W. Greg. Oxford: Oxford University Press, 1907.

————. *The Scottish History of James IV.* In *The Revels Plays*, edited by Norman Sanders. London: Methuen, 1970.

Heywood, Thomas. *The First and Second Parts of King Edward the Fourth.* Facsimile reprint of the first edition in the library of Charles W. Clark. Philadelphia: The Rosenbach Co., 1922.

————. *The English Traveller; The Wise Woman of Hoxton.* In *Three Marriage Plays*, edited by Paul Merchant. Manchester: Manchester University Press, 1996.

Jonson, Ben. *Bartholomew Fair.* In *The Selected Plays of Ben Jonson*, edited by Martin Butler. Cambridge: Cambridge University Press, 1989.

————. *Cataline His Conspiracy.* In *The Complete Plays of Ben Jonson*, edited by G. A. Wilkes. Oxford: Clarendon Press, 1982.

————. *Cynthia's Revels.* In *Ben Jonson*, edited by C. H. Herford and Percy Simpson. Oxford: Clarendon Press, 1931; repr. 1954.

————. *Sejanus His Fall.* In *The Revels Plays*, edited by Philip Ayres. Manchester: Manchester University Press, 1990.

Kyd, Thomas. *The Spanish Tragedy.* In *The Revels Plays*, edited by Philip Edwards. London: Methuen, 1959; repr. 1969.

Lyly, John. *Endymion.* In *The Revels Plays*, edited by David Bevington. Manchester: Manchester University Press, 1996.

————. *Mother Bombie.* In *Malone Society Reprints*, edited by Kathleen M. Lee and D. Nichols. Oxford: Oxford University Press, 1948 for 1939.

————. *Sappho and Phao.* In *John Lyly, Campaspe and Sappho and Phao*, edited by George K. Hunter and David Bevington. Manchester: Manchester University Press, 1991.

Marlowe, Christopher, *Dido Queen of Carthage.* In *The Revels Plays*, edited by H. J. Oliver. London: Methuen, 1960.

_____. *The Massacre At Paris*. In *The Revels Plays*, edited by H. J. Oliver. London: Methuen, 1968.

Marston, John. *Antonio's Revenge*. In *The Revels Plays*, edited by Reavley Gair. Manchester: Manchester University Press, 1978.

_____. *Sophonisba*. In *The Selected Plays of John Marston*, edited by Macdonald P. Jackson and Michael Neill. Cambridge: Cambridge University Press, 1986.

_____. *The Dutch Courtesan*. In *Fountainwell Drama Texts*, edited by Peter Davison. Edinburgh: Oliver and Boyd, 1968.

_____. *The Malcontent*. In *The Revels Plays*, edited by George K. Hunter. Manchester: Manchester University Press, 1975.

Mason, John. *The Turk*. Edited by Fernand Lagarde. Salzburg: Universitat Salzburg, 1979.

Massinger, Philip. *The Plays and Poems of Philip Massinger*. 2 vols. Edited by Philip Edwards and Colin Gibson. Oxford: Clarendon Press, 1976.

Middleton, John. *A Chaste Maid In Cheapside*. In *The Revels Plays*, edited by R. B. Parker. Manchester: Manchester University Press, 1984.

Middleton, Thomas. *No Wit, No Help Like a Woman's*. In *Regents Renaissance Drama Series*, edited by Lowell E. Johnson. Lincoln: University of Nebraska Press, 1976.

_____. *A Mad World My Masters*. Edited by Michael Taylor. Oxford: Oxford University Press, 1995.

_____. *Michaelmas Term*. In *The Revels Plays*, edited by Gail Kern Paster. Manchester: Manchester University Press, 2000.

_____. *The Phoenix*. Edited by John Bradbury Brooks. New York: Garland Publishing, 1980.

_____. *The Puritan or The Widow of Watling Street*. In *The Shakespeare Apocrypha*, edited by C. F. Tucker Brooke. Oxford: Clarendon Press, 1908; repr. 1967.

_____. *The Revenger's Tragedy*. In *The Revels Plays.*, edited by R. A. Foakes. London: Methuen, 1966. This edition attributes authorship to Cyril Tourneur.

_____. *The Witch*. In *New Mermaids*, edited by Elizabeth Schafer. London: A & C Black, 1994.

Middleton, Thomas and William Rowley. *A Fair Quarrel*. In *Regents Renaissance Drama Series*, edited by George R. Price. London: Edward Arnold, 1977.

Munday, Anthony. *John a Kent and John a Cumber*. In *Malone Society Reprints*, edited by Muriel St Clare Byrne. Oxford: Oxford University Press, 1923.

_____. *The Downfall of Robert Earl of Huntingdon*. In *Malone Society Reprints*, edited by John C. Meagler and Arthur Brown. Oxford: Oxford University Press, 1965 for 1964.

Peele, George. *Edward I*. In *The Dramatic Works of George Peele*, edited by Frank S. Hook. New Haven and London: Yale University Press, 1961.

_____. *The Old Wives' Tale*. In *The Revel Plays*, edited by Patricia Binnie. Manchester: Manchester University Press, 1980.

Phillip, John. *The Play of Patient Grissil*. In *Malone Society Reprints*, edited by Ronald B. McKerrow and W. W. Greg. Oxford: Oxford University Press, 1909.

Porter, Henry. *The Two Angry Women of Abingdon*. Edited by Michael Jardine and John Simons. Nottingham: Nottingham Drama Texts, 1987.

R. B. *Appius and Virginia*. In *Malone Society Reprints*, edited by Ronald B. McKerrow and W. W. Greg. London: Chiswick Press, 1911.

Shakespeare, William. *The Complete Works, Oxford Edition*, edited by Stanley Wells and Gary Taylor. Oxford: Oxford University Press, 1988.

————. *All's Well That Ends Well*. Edited by Barbara Everett. Harmondsworth: Penguin, 1970.

Stevenson, William (?). *Gammer Gurton's Needle*. In *New Mermaids*, edited by Charles Whitworth. 2nd edn. London: A & C Black, 1997.

Webster, John. *The White Devil*. In *The Revels Plays*, edited by John Russell Brown. London: Methuen, 1960; 2nd edn 1966.

Books

Adelman, Janet. *Suffocating Mothers: Fantasies of Maternal Origin In Shakespeare's Plays, Hamlet to The Tempest*. New York: Routledge, 1992.

Aughterson, Kate, ed. *Renaissance Women: Constructions of Femininity in England*. London: Routledge, 1995.

Barry, Jonathan, ed. *The Tudor and Stuart Town: A Reader in English Urban History*. London: Longman, 1990.

Bell, Maureen, George Parfitt and Simon Shepherd, eds. *A Biographical Dictionary of English Women Writers*. London: Harvester Wheatsheaf, 1990.

Borman, Tracy. *Elizabeth's Women: The Hidden Story of the Virgin Queen*. London: Jonathan Cape, 2009.

Bradford, Charles Angel. *Blanche Parry, Queen Elizabeth's Gentlewoman*. London: R. F. Hunger, 1935.

Brown, Pamela Allen. *Better a Shrew Than a Sheep: Women, Drama and the Culture of Jest in Early Modern England*. Ithaca and London: Cornell University Press, 2003.

Callaghan, Dympna, ed. *A Feminist Companion to Shakespeare*. Oxford: Blackwell, 1994.

Callaghan, Dympna, Lorraine Helms and Jyotsna Singh, eds. *The Weyward Sisters: Shakespeare and Feminist Politics*. Oxford: Blackwell, 1994.

Campbell, Erin, ed. *Growing Old in Early Modern Europe Cultural Representations*. Aldershot: Ashgate, 2006.

Clarke, Danielle and Elizabeth Clarke, eds. *'This Double Voice': Gendered Writing in Early Modern England*. Basingstoke: Macmillan, 2000.

Clifford, H., ed. *The Diaries of Anne Clifford*. Stroud: Allan Sutton, 1990.

BIBLIOGRAPHY

Cobb, Christopher J. *The Staging of Romance in Late Shakespeare Text and Theatrical Technique*. Newark: University of Delaware Press, 2007.

Copeman, W. S. C. *Doctors and Disease in Tudor Time*. London: Dawson, 1960.

Corum, Richard. *Understanding Hamlet: A Student Casebook to Issues, Sources, and Historical Documents*. Westport, CT: Greenwood Press, 1998.

Cox, John D. and David Scott Kaston, eds. *A New History of Early English Drama*. New York: Columbia University Press, 1997.

Crawford, Patricia and Laura Gowing. *Women's Worlds in Seventeenth-Century England*. London: Routledge, 2000.

Crawford, Patricia. *Blood, Bodies and Family in Early Modern England*. Harlow: Pearson Education, 2004.

Deats, Sara Munson, ed. *Antony and Cleopatra: New Critical Essays*. Abingdon: Routledge, 2005.

de Bruyn, Lucy. *Woman and The Devil in Sixteenth-Century Literature*. Tisbury: The Compton Press, 1979.

de Lisle, Leanda. *After Elizabeth: How James King of Scots Won the Crown of England in 1603*. London: Harper Collins, 2005.

Dolan, Frances E. *Dangerous Familiars: Representations of Domestic Crime in England 1550–1700*. Ithaca: Cornell University Press, 1994.

Donnison, Jean. *Midwives and Medical Men: A History of the Struggle for the Control of Childbirth*. New Barnet: Historical Publications, 1988.

Elden, George S., ed. *The Description of England*. William Harrison. Ithaca: Cornell University Press, 1968.

Ellis, Henry, ed. *Ellis's Original Letters*. 2nd series. London: Harding and Leopard, 1827.

Emmison, F. G. *Elizabethan Life: Disorder*. Chelmsford: Essex County Council, 1970.

Erickson, Amy Louise. *Women and Property in Early Modern England*. London: Routledge, 1993.

Faulkner, Thomas C., Nicolas K. Kiessling and Rhonda L. Blair, eds. *The Anatomy of Melancholy*. Vol. 3. Oxford: Clarendon Press, 1994.

Froide, Amy M. *Never Married Singlewomen in Early Modern England*. Oxford: Oxford University Press, 2005.

Frye, Susan and Karen Robertson. *Maids and Mistresses, Cousins and Queens: Women's Alliances in Early Modern England*. Oxford: Oxford University Press, 1999.

Gibson, Marion. *Reading Witchcraft: Stories of Early English Witches*. London: Routledge, 1999.

Goreau, Angeline, ed. *The Whole Duty of a Woman: Female Writers In Seventeenth-Century England*. New York: The Dial Press, 1985.

Gowing, Laura. *Common Bodies, Women, Touch and Power in Seventeenth-Century England*. New Haven and London: Yale University Press, 2003.

Green, Gayle, and Carol Neely, eds. *The Woman's Part: Feminist Criticism of Shakespeare*. Urbana: University of Illinois Press, 1980.

Griffiths, John, ed. *The Two Books of Homilies Appointed to be Read in the Churches*. Oxford: Oxford University Press, 1859.

Haselkorn, Anne M. *Prostitution in Elizabethan and Jacobean Comedy*. Troy: The Whitston Publishing Company, 1983.

Henderson, Katherine Usher and Barbara F. McManus, eds. *Half Humankind: Contexts and Texts of the Controversy about Women in 1580–1640*. Chicago: University of Chicago Press, 1985.

Hester, Marianne. *Lewd Women and Wicked Witches: A Study of the Dynamics of Male Domination*. London: Routledge, 1992.

Houlbrooke, Ralph A. *The English Family 1450–1700*. London: Longman, 1984.

Howard, Jean E., and Marion F. O'Connor, eds. *Shakespeare Reproduced: The Text in History and Ideology*. New York: Methuen, 1987.

Hughey, Ruth, ed. *The Correspondence of Lady Katherine Paston 1602–1627*. Norfolk: The Norfolk Recording Society, 1941.

Hull, Suzanne W., ed. *Chaste, Silent and Obedient: English Books for Women 1475 1640*. San Marino: Huntington Library, 1962.

Hunt, Maurice, ed. *The Winter's Tale Critical Essays*. London: Garland Publishing, 1995.

Hunter, Lynette and Sarah Hutton, eds. *Women, Science and Medicine 1500–1700: Mothers and Sisters of the Royal Society*. Stroud: Sutton Publishing, 1997.

James I. *Basilicon Doron (1599)*. Menston: The Scolar Press, 1969.

Jardine, Lisa and Alan Stewart. *Hostage to Fortune: The Troubled Life of Francis Bacon*. London: Victor Gollantz, 1998.

Jowett, John, William Montgomery, Gary Taylor and Stanley Wells, eds. *The Oxford Shakespeare: The Complete Works*. 2nd edn. Oxford: Clarendon Press, 2006.

Kahn, Coppelia. *Roman Shakespeare: Warriors, Wounds and Women*. London: Routledge, 1997.

Kehler, Dorothea and Susan Barker, eds. *In Another Country: Feminist Perspectives on Renaissance Drama*. Metuchen, NJ: The Scarecrow Press, 1991.

Kelso, Ruth. *Doctrine for the Lady of the Renaissance*. Urbana: University of Illinois Press, 1956.

Kinney, Arthur F., ed. *Hamlet New Critical Essays*. London: Routledge 2002.

Korda, Natasha. *Shakespeare's Domestic Economies Gender and Property in Early Modern England*. Philadelphia: University of Pennsylvania Press, 2002.

Krueger, Robert, ed. *The Poems of Sir John Davies*. Oxford: Clarendon Press, 1975.

Laslett, Peter. *The World We Have Lost:Further Explored*. London, Methuen, 1983.

Leech, Clifford. *The John Fletcher Plays*. London: Chatto and Windus, 1962.

Levack, Brian P. *The Witch-Hunt in Early Modern Europe*. London: Pearson Education, 2006.

Levin, Carole and Patricia A. Sullivan, eds. *Political Rhetoric, Power and Renaissance Women*. Albany: State University of New York Press, 1995.

Levy Peck, Linda, ed. *The Mental World of the Jacobean Court*. Cambridge: Cambridge University Press, 2005.

Lovell, Mary S. *Bess of Hardwick First Lady of Chatsworth 1527–1608*. London: Little, Brown, 2005.

Macdonald, Michael. *Mystical Bedlam: Madness, Anxiety and Healing in Seventeenth-Century England*. Cambridge: Cambridge University Press, 1981.

Macfarlane, Alan. *Witchcraft in Tudor and Stuart England: A Regional and Comparative Study*. London: Routledge and Kegan Paul, 1970.

Macintosh, Marjorie Keniston. *A Community Transformed: The Manor and Liberty of Havering 1500–1620*. Cambridge: Cambridge University Press, 1991.

Maclean, John, ed. *Letters from George Lord Carew to Sir Thomas Roe Ambassador to the Court of the Great Mogul 1615–1617*. London: The Camden Society, 1860.

————, ed. *The Berkeley Manuscripts: The Lives of the Berkeleys by John Smyth of Nibley*. Vol. 2. Gloucester: Bristol and Gloucestershire Archaeological Society, 1933.

Maley, Willy and Margaret Tudeau-Clayton, eds. *This England, That Shakespeare: New Angles on Englishness and the Bard*. Farnham: Ashgate, 2010.

Mashburn, Joseph H. and Alec R. Velie, eds. *Blood and Knavery: A Collection of English Renaissance Ballads of Crime and Sin*. Cranbury, NJ: Associated University Presses, 1973.

Mendelson, Sara and Patricia Crawford. *Women In Early Modern England 1550–1720*. Oxford: Clarendon Press, 1998.

Moncrief, Kathryn M., and Kathryn R. McPherson, eds. *Performing Maternity in Early Modern England*. Aldershot: Ashgate, 2007.

Nichols, John Gough, ed. *The Diary of Henry Machyn Citizen and Merchant Taylor of London from AD 1550–AD 1563*. London: Camden Society, 1848.

Ostovich, Helen and Elizabeth Sauer, eds., assisted by Melissa Smith. *Reading Early Modern Women: An Anthology of Texts in Manuscript and Print 1550–1700*. Routledge: London, 2004.

Outhwaite, R. B., ed. *Marriage and Society: Studies in the Social History of Marriage*. London: Europa, 1981.

Palliser, D. M. *The Age of Elizabeth: England Under the Later Tudors 1547–1603*. London: Longman, 1992.

Paylor, W. J., ed. *The Overburian Characters to Which Is Added A Wife*. Oxford: Basil Blackwell, 1936.

Pelling, Margaret and Richard M. Smith, eds. *Life, Death and the Elderly: Historical Perspectives*. London: Routledge, 1991.

Pendry, E. D., ed. *The Wonderful Year and Selected Writings*. London: Edward Arnold, 1969.

Pollock, Linda. *With Faith and Physic: The Life of a Tudor Gentlewoman Lady Grace Mildmay 1552–1620*. London: Collins and Brown, 1993.

Prior, Mary, ed. *Women in English Society 1500–1800*. London: Methuen, 1985.

Rappaport, Steve. *Worlds Within Worlds: Structures of Life in Sixteenth-Century London*. Cambridge: Cambridge University Press, 1989.

Rye, William Brenchley, ed. *England As Seen by Foreigners in the Days of Elizabeth and James the First*. New York: Benjamin Blom, 1967.

Sharp, David and Sean Delaney, eds. *Women in Feature Films: A Research Guide About Representations of Women Over 60*. London: U3A and BFI, 2006.

Smith, Richard M., ed. *Land, Kinship and the Life-Cycle*. Cambridge: Cambridge University Press, 1984.

Somerset, Anne. *Ladies in Waiting: From the Tudors to the Present Day*. London: Weidenfeld and Nicholson, 1984.

Spedding, James, ed. *The Letters and Life of Francis Bacon*. Vol. 4. London: Longmans, Green, Reader and Dyer, 1868.

St Clare Byrne, Muriel. *The Lisle Letters*. Vol. 1. Chicago: University of Chicago Press, 1981.

Statham, Edward Phillips, ed. *A Jacobean Letter-Writer: The Life and Times of John Chamberlain*. London: Kegan Paul, Trench, Trubner, 1921.

Stretton, Tim. *Women Waging Law in Elizabethan England*. Cambridge: Cambridge University Press, 1988.

Strong, Roy. *The Cult of Elizabeth: Elizabethan Portraiture and Pagentry*. 2nd edn. London: Pimlico, 1999.

Thane, Pat. *Old Age in English History: Past Experiences, Present Issues*. Oxford: Oxford University Press, 2000.

Towler, Jean, and Joan Bramall. *Midwives in History and Society*. London: Croom Helm, 1986.

Warnicke, Retha M. *Women of the English Renaissance and Reformation*. London: Greenwood Press, 1983.

Weisner, Merry, E. *Women and Gender in Early Modern Europe*. Cambridge: Cambridge University Press, 2000.

Wells, Stanley. *Shakespeare & Co*. London: Penguin 2007.

Wiltenberg, Joy. *Disorderly Women and Female Power in the Street Literature of Early Modern England and Germany*. Charlottesville: University Press of Virginia, 1992.

Zunder, William and Suzanne Trill eds. *Writing and the English Renaissance*. London: Longman, 1996.

Journals

Borthwick Papers 58 (1980)
Continuity and Change 8 (1993)

Criminal Justice History 6 (1985)
English Literary Renaissance 22 (1992)
History 75 (1990)
History of Education 23 (1994)
The Historian 46 (1984)
International Journal of Women's Studies 6 (1993)
Literature and Belief 2 (1982)
Medical History 28 (1984)
MHRA Working Papers in the Humanities 1 (2006)
Sixteenth Century Journal 19 (1988)
The Society for the Social History of Medicine 20 (1990)
Studies in English Literature 22 (1982)
United Nations Division for the Advancement of Women (2002)

Microfilms

Beard, Thomas. *The Theatre of God's Judgements or a Collection of True Stories. Tr. Out of French and Augmented by T. Beard*. London, 1597.
Cuffe, Henry. *The Differences of the Ages of Man's Life*. London, 1600.
Day, John. *The Ile of Guls. As it Hath Been Often Playd*. London, 1606.
Goulart, Simon. *The Wise Veillard, or Old Man. Tr. Out of French by (T. W[illiamson?])*. London, 1621.
Reading, John. *The Old Man's Staffe, Two Sermons*. London, 1621.
S. S. *The Honest Lawyer*. London, 1616.
Stubbes, Philip. *The Anatomie of Abuses*. London, 1583.

Websites

Gardner, Lyn. 'Margaret Tyzack: The Accidental Actor'. *Guardian*. 23 June 2009. http://www.guardian.co.uk/stage/2009/jun/23/Margaret-tyzack/print. Accessed 24 April 2013.
Griffiths, Ian J. 'Older Women Unhappy Over Portrayal in Films, Survey Shows'. *Guardian*. 28 March 2011. http://www.guardian.co.uk/fil/2011/mar/28. Accessed 24 April 2013.
Hill, Amelia. 'Women, Gay and Black People Still Shown as Stereotypes in Film, Says Study'. *Guardian*. 18 March 2011. Accessed 24 April 2013.
Walter, Harriet. 'Why Do Stories Never Involve Women Over 50?'. *Guardian*. 18 March 2011. http://www.guardian.co.uk/fil/2011/mar/18. Accessed 24 April 2013.
'Woman's Hour'. BBC. May 2006. http://www.bbc.co.uk/radio4/womanshour03/2006. Accessed 24 April 2013.